Poem of My Cid
(Selections)

Poema de Mio Cid
(Selección)

A Dual-Language Book

Edited and Translated by

STANLEY APPELBAUM

DOVER PUBLICATIONS, INC.
Mineola, New York

Bibliographical Note

This Dover edition, first published in 2005, is a new selection of entire strophes (including a total of 2,422 verses out of 3,735) from the work first published in 1779 (the specific edited text was published in 1913; see Introduction for details), together with a new English translation of the material selected, summaries of the omitted strophes, an Introduction, and footnotes, all prepared by Stanley Appelbaum.

Library of Congress Cataloging-in-Publication Data

Cantar de mío Cid. English & Spanish. Selections.
    Poem of my Cid : selections = Poema de mio Cid : selección / edited and translated by Stanley Appelbaum.
        p. cm. — (A dual-language book)
    ISBN 0-486-44016-8 (pbk.)
        1. Cid, ca. 1043–1099—Romances. I. Title: Poema de mio Cid. II. Appelbaum, Stanley. III. Title. IV. Series.

PQ6367.E3A66 2005
861'.1—dc22

                                                                2004061767

Manufactured in the United States of America
Dover Publications, Inc., 31 East 2nd Street, Mineola, N.Y. 11501

INTRODUCTION

The Christian Visigothic kingdom in Spain, which had been established in A.D. 415, was wiped out by Islamized Berbers ("Moors") invading from North Africa, beginning in 711. The emirate founded in Córdoba in 755 (transformed into a caliphate independent of Baghdad in 929) ruled all of Moorish Spain until 1031, when Islamic territory split up into a number of petty states (this was the situation in the Cid's lifetime; the puritanical Berber Almoravids, who began to invade Spain in 1086, reunified the Moorish lands there by 1110).

Meanwhile, the unconquered Christians in Asturias began the slow Reconquest in the 720s, and by 910 their northwestern and north central territory was divided into Asturias, León, and Galicia. Castile, a frontier region of León on the border with the separate kingdom of Navarre (the northeast, including Aragon and Catalonia, was developing independently), became a county (domain of a count) in 946. Fernando I (born ca. 1016) became count of Castile in 1029 and king of León-Asturias-Galicia in 1038. When he died in 1065, he dismembered his realm in a Lear-like fashion, leaving his eldest son, Sancho II (born ca. 1038), as king of Castile; his second son, Alfonso VI (born 1040), as king of León; and his youngest son, García, as king of Galicia. Sancho and Alfonso joined forces to dethrone García, then the still dissatisfied Sancho drove Alfonso into exile. In 1072, while Sancho was besieging his sister Urraca's apanage, the city of Zamora, he was killed treacherously, and Alfonso returned to rule over his father's entire reconstituted territory. The greatest success of his reign was the conquest of Toledo in 1085 (though it was this victory that brought the fierce Almoravids to Spain at the invitation of the frightened petty emirs);[1] Alfonso died in 1109.

---

1. The Almoravid ruler was Yusuf ibn Teshufin (1009–1106), whose reign began in 1061; he founded Marrakesh in 1062. Yusuf is the only Moor named in the *Poema de Mio Cid* who is definitely historical.

The outstanding Spanish military genius of this second half of the eleventh century was Rodrigo (Ruy)[2] Díaz, lord of Vivar (a village about five miles north of Burgos; the monastery of San Pedro de Cárdenas, where he was buried, was founded in 899 and is just a few miles southeast of the same city). Born ca. 1043, Rodrigo received the honorary Arabic title of the Cid ("lord, master") because of his exploits among the Moors. At one time his true existence was doubted, but there are numerous archival documents bearing his name. He was an *infanzón,* a member of the minor nobility from the borderlands, often self-made men, who were held in contempt by the *ricos hombres,* the long-settled, land-rich upper nobility of the León heartland. The Cid was probably not a descendant of former rulers of Castile. He was brought up by crown prince Sancho (later Sancho II), whom he probably served in a minor capacity, not as chief standard-bearer; his wife Jimena was probably not the niece of a count, related to royalty.

He was exiled by Alfonso VI on two occasions. The first exile (1081–1087) was decreed either because he had raided Toledo territory (not yet conquered by Alfonso, but already the king's ally), or because, while on a tribute-collecting mission in Seville, he defeated Alfonso's favorite, Garci Ordóñez, who had attacked Seville in behalf of another Moorish realm. During this first exile, the Cid found no employment in Barcelona (a cause of later resentment?—twice, in 1082 and 1090, he captured the count of Barcelona, Berenguer Ramón II, "the fratricide" [1053–1097; ruled 1076–1096]), and subsequently entered the service of the emir of Zaragoza (obviously, at this time Moors and Christians were not prevented from cooperating by intense religious or patriotic considerations). Reconciled to the king after defeating Yusuf, the Cid ran afoul of him again in 1089 for failing to respond to a summons to battle; thereafter, he began to seek Valencia as a personal, not royal, conquest. He finally captured that realm (which contains the most fertile land in Spain) in 1094, holding it until his death in 1099. (It was lost again, to the Almoravids, in 1102, and had to be reconquered from the Moors in 1238 by the king of Aragon; it is still in the northeastern Iberian sphere of influence, the local language being a variety of Catalan.)

In 1097 the Cid's son Diego (not mentioned in the *Poema*) died

---

2. Given names immediately followed by a patronymic ("family name") were frequently shortened in older Spanish; thus: Fernán González = Fernando (son) of Gonzalo. Other examples in the *Poema* are: García (but Garci Ordóñez) and Álvar (for Álvaro) Fáñez; Álvar Fáñez's nickname Minaya seems to be a combination of Castilian *mi* ("my") and Basque *anaia* ("brother").

fighting for Alfonso. In 1098 his daughters Cristina and María (not Elvira and Sol, as in the *Poema,* though those might possibly have been secondary names) married, respectively, the crown prince of Navarre (who, through circumstances, never got to reign) and the count of Barcelona. By about 1200, various Spanish royal lines were descended in some measure from the Cid.

Rodrigo's fame soon spawned legend. Latin poems about him may have begun appearing during his lifetime (the dates of extant fragments are hotly disputed). A Latin prose *Historia Roderici* (1115? 1140s?) is the best source of reliable information, though it is being used more cautiously all the time. During the era (14th–16th centuries) when the *romances viejos* (older traditional ballads) were being written, some 200 were devoted to the Cid's career.[3]

In addition, in the 13th–16th centuries the legend of the Cid was expanded to enormous length in Spanish-language prose chronicles devoted to general history or to the Cid alone. About 1370 (though it may be a recasting of older material) there appeared an epic poem (only partially preserved) about the *mocedades* (youthful exploits) of the Cid; it is this legendary early phase of his life, especially his marriage to the orphaned Jimena, which was the basis of major 17th-century plays in Spain and France.

But by far the most important literary work related to the Cid is the *Poema de Mio Cid* (also known as the *Cantar de Mio Cid,* though "*cantar*" is ambiguous, also referring to perceived subdivisions of the work). The *Poema* is the only virtually complete Castilian epic poem that has come down to us in its essentially original form.[4] Unfortunately, almost everything about it is enveloped in uncertainty, and even individual scholars change their minds about crucial aspects of the problems. So many new ideas have surfaced in recent decades

3. Besides elaborating on incidents in the *Poema,* these ballads (in form, like strophes of the *Poema*) celebrate many legends that must have sprung up subsequently, such as: Jimena asking Alfonso to marry her to Rodrigo after he had killed her father for insulting his own father; the Cid's acts of insubordination to Alfonso, especially the harshly worded oath he forced the king to swear, to the effect that he had had no part in the murder of his brother Sancho at Zamora; the appearance of Saint Peter to the Cid, announcing his death; and the victory over Moors won by the Cid's corpse, strapped to his horse. Four of the oldest and best Cid *romances* are included in the Dover dual-language volume (same editor/translator as this one) *Spanish Traditional Ballads/Romances viejos españoles,* 2003 (ISBN 0-486-42694-7).   4. Other remains of early Spanish epic are either extremely fragmentary (such as *Roncesvalles*), or fragmentary and late (such as the *Mocedades*), or recast in a later type of verse form (such as the *Fernán González* poem), or else assumed to have existed because what must have been old epic verses are embedded in various prose chronicles.

that a 1968 introduction to the *Poema* (still in print) is completely out of date.

The *Poema* is preserved in a single quarto manuscript, which was discovered in Vivar late in the 16th century; after passing through many private hands, it was acquired in 1960 by the Biblioteca Nacional in Madrid. The *Poema* (along with several other major medieval works) was first published in 1779 in Thomas [*sic*] Antonio Sánchez's *Colección de poesías castellanas anteriores al siglo XV* (Collection of Castilian Poems Earlier Than the 15th Century), published by Antonio de Sancha, Madrid (the *Poema* is in the first of four volumes; the fourth appeared as late as 1790).[5] Everyone agrees that the MS is written in a 14th-century hand, but that the text is much earlier. There is great controversy over the original date of composition. It was once an article of faith, but is no longer so, that Spanish epics were written soon after the events they narrate, and were essentially realistic and true to history; thus, the *Poema* was seen as basically an early 12th-century product, and apparent anachronisms were explained away by an elaborate theory of subsequent recastings (also, every editor has had a specific Spanish political event or trend to cite in support of the date he has favored). Some important scholars now believe that the beginning of the 13th century is the correct date, but, if there is any general leaning at present, it is toward the late 12th century, on the basis of such elements as the judicial practices described in the poem, as well as its language.[6] The question of date is also closely associated with the equally puzzling one of authorship.

---

5. Those unaccustomed to the ways of Academe might imagine that, given a single manuscript source, the text of the *Poema* (except for introduced modernizations) would be the same in every edition. Nothing could be further from the truth. First of all, the MS is hard to read, its deterioration having chiefly been caused by earlier "curators" who treated it with chemicals that blackened large sections. But, above all else, the very absence of other MSS which might confirm difficult readings, providing a "consensus," has provoked editors into making all sorts of personal emendations. This practice was at its height in the early 20th century, whereas the current trend is to restore as many as possible of the MS's peculiarities (bad assonance, partial lines, unusual word forms, etc.), partly on the assumption that the MS copyist(s) just couldn't have made that many mistakes—though, in view of all the typos in modern Spanish scholarly editions, one is sorely tempted to retort: "Oh, no?" 6. Unlike French, English, and German of the same period, early Castilian can be read, with just a little self-preparation, by good readers of today's Spanish; there is no need to study it as virtually a separate language. Aside from obvious, and not alarming, differences in spelling and vowel color, and a few metatheses of consonants, as well as its share of words now obsolete, archaic, or of altered semantic meanings, the language of the *Poema* is largely characterized by such features as: the retention of etymological verb endings from Latin (e.g., in *ganades;* modern *ganáis*); the loss of *-e* in the weak pro-

Besides the question of single versus multiple authorship, the question of later revisions, and the question of disruptive manipulation by practicing minstrels of an originally more regular literary text, one must consider the last five verses (3731–3735) in the MS. The first three of these, in the same hand as verses 1–3730, state that in the year 1207 (for many years, read as 1307, which raised even more difficulties) a man named Per (Pedro) Abbat *escrivió* the foregoing poem. Almost everyone now believes that *escrivió* means "copied out," not "composed," though one scholar, who later recanted, established an elaborate, archivally based, biography of Per Abbat. (The last two lines in the MS are obviously by a minstrel of some period, who says he has now finished the recitation and requests money, or payment in kind, from his listeners.) Many recent scholars believe in an initial composition by a single, well-educated person who knew a lot about legal terminology and practice.

The *Poema* resembles the earliest French epic poems, which may not have preceded it by very long, in consisting of strophes (*laisses* in French; *tiradas* or *series* in Spanish) of greatly varying lengths (3 to almost 200 verses), all the verses in a given strophe ending in more or less the same one- or two-syllable assonances (e.g., in strophe 1, every line ends with two syllables, in the first of which (the stressed one) the vowel is *a,* and in the second of which it is *o*). The number of syllables per verse, however, is extremely irregular in the *Poema,* as is the position within the verse of the caesura, or natural breathing space (in some verses its position even being a subject of dispute among scholars). Reflecting a genuine oral verse-narrative tradition (or perhaps simulating it?), the author(s) made extensive use of repeated formulas and epithets (e.g., "the excellent man from Burgos"). The narrative is not evenly continuous, but selects outstanding moments.

Controversy extends even to the possible subdivisions of the work. Most editors place the heading *"Cantar primero"* ("First Canto") at the beginning, and introduce a *segundo* with strophe 64, and a *tercero* with strophe 112. The chief basis for the break at strophe 64 is its first verse (verse 1085), which reads: "Here begins the *gesta* of My Cid, lord of

---

nouns *me, te, le,* and *se,* with the subsequent attachment of the remaining letter to the preceding word (e.g., *veot;* modern *te veo*); and the frequent "separation" of the *haber*-derived "endings" of the "future" and "conditional" tenses from the infinitive "stem" of the verb (e.g., *conbidar le ien;* modern *le convidarían*). Roughly speaking, in pronunciation, the modern English equivalents of -*s*- (between vowels); *x; j,* and *g* before *e* or *i; ç,* and *c* before *e* and *i;* and *z* would be, respectively: *z; sh; s* as in "measure"; *ts;* and *dz* as in "adze."

Vivar"; but many believe that *"gesta"* here does not mean a canto, but an exploit, *the* principal exploit: the taking of Valencia. The break at strophe 112 is much more justified, because strophe 111 clearly ends with a rather lengthy direct address of the author (or performer) to the (real or imagined) audience. The presence of only two subdivisions would also suit the purposes of those scholars who find a binary division in every aspect of the poem, the overall one being between the Cid's military successes and his later family and civil successes.

Earlier critics stressed the historicity of the poem, but their ground has slowly crumbled away. As mentioned above, Yusuf is a real historical character, as are Garci Ordóñez and Álvar Fáñez. But Garci Ordóñez probably never did as much as he is called on to do in the poem, and it seems that Álvar Fáñez, far from being the Cid's "right arm," had little to do with him and was a loyal captain of Alfonso's; he was most likely drafted by the author(s) into his sidekick status because of his fame as the second greatest military leader or *condottiere* after the Cid in the same generation. On the other hand, many major characters and events are totally fictitious: Martín Antolínez is probably an invention glorifying the city of Burgos, the metropolis of the oldest Castile before its huge expansion; whereas there is no historical record whatsoever of the young lords of Carrión or of a marriage of the Cid's daughter before the ones narrated at the very end of the poem!

True, there is much less fantasy in the *Poema* than in some of the French epics. Even the apparition of the archangel Gabriel is narrated as a mere dream, though a prophetic one. Religion does not weigh too heavily on the action; even the first bishop of Valencia (the historical Jérôme of Périgord) is depicted as a warrior priest (a common phenomenon in medieval epics and ballads; cf. Friar Tuck in the Robin Hood cycle); while great attention is paid to such mundane matters as financing a campaign, obtaining provisions, and especially gaining booty. The actual coexistence between Christians and Moors at the time (a sort of armed truce except for very specific hostilities) is clearly reflected. On the other hand, there are several elements in the narrative that are blatantly folkloric, such as the substitution of sand for valuables in locked chests.[7] And the entire *Poema* is enlivened with a great deal of brisk dialogue and a wide-ranging appeal to the emotions, from humor to heartbreak.

---

7. The moneylenders on whom this trick is played in the *Poema* are most likely Jews (they are clearly identified as such in the related ballads and chronicles). The name Vidas is thought by some to represent the Hebrew name of similar meaning, Chayim.

Like most serious medieval literature, the *Poema* is also didactic, in that it proposes a shining model for living one's life: the Cid. Loyal to an overlord who spurns him, so lawabiding as to prefer a public weighing of his grievances to a private feud, sensitive and kind not only to his own followers but also to the Moors when he governs, just and generous, and almost always levelheaded, moderate, and prudent (the only two impetuous actions imputed to him are kicking the door in Burgos and—sometime in the past—plucking García's beard), the Cid is a paragon of knighthood and gentlemanly behavior. But he is not portrayed as a "stick": many of his utterances are witty, ironic, or even sarcastic, and he has a bright, optimistic personality. Another particularly upright character in the *Poema* is Ibn Ghaldun, the friendly and loyal emir of Molina de Aragón, who has been called the first "noble Moor" in what later became a tradition in Spanish literature (cf. the "noble savage" of the New World in European writing of the 16th century and afterward).

This Dover edition includes, in both the original text and a new English translation, 65% of the *Poema* (2,422 verses out of 3,735), with reasonably full English summaries of the sections omitted. Without exception, every strophe included in the fully presented sections is complete, no matter how long it may be. The Spanish text is essentially the one established by the great scholar Ramón Menéndez Pidal in his 1913 edition of the *Poema* ("Clásicos Castellanos," Espasa-Calpe, Madrid). His Spanish text is intentionally regularized to a greater extent than in present-day practice, evening out many of the manuscript's anomalies in assonance, length and sequence of verses, and the like. His italics (retained in this Dover edition) indicate material he added (out of a variety of considerations), ranging from a single letter to a series of verses (using chronicle texts to supply information perceived as missing from the *Poema* MS). His text, still in print after setting a standard for most of the 20th century, is very helpful to beginners in medieval studies and is appropriate in an introductory volume like this Dover edition.[8]

---

8. Those eager and ready to confront modern critical texts, with a battery of apparatus, should consult the complete editions of the *Poema* by Colin Smith ("Letras Hispánicas," Cátedra, Madrid, 20th ed., 1996) and Ian Michael ("Clásicos Castalia," Editorial Castalia, Madrid, 5th ed., 1991). A helpful running commentary on cultural features, especially enlightening in such technical areas as the jurisprudence reflected in the *cortes* at Toledo, is to be found in the edition (called *Cantar de Mio Cid*) by José Luis Girón Alconchel and María Virginia Pérez Escribano ("Castalia Didáctica," Editorial Castalia, Madrid, 1995).

In the present volume, the strophes are numbered as they tradi-
tionally are (but are not given editorial headings based on their con-
tent), whereas verse numbers are indicated only for large groupings,
not by clusters of five verses, as in many editions. Following the MS
practice, there is no subdivision into two or three *cantares,* and the
caesuras (sometimes controversial) are not indicated by additional
space. The translation is strictly line-for-line, and often reflects the
translator's considered choice among a variety of possible meanings
(an intentionally very small sampling of such ambiguities is offered in
footnotes to the respective passages). Three recent commented texts,
as well as one full translation into present-day Spanish, were con-
sulted. Other footnotes are intended merely as immediate, on-the-
spot aids to comprehension. Not all personal and (real) geographical
names are glossed (a good, indexed map of Spain is recommended to
those who wish to follow the narrative and this Introduction in geo-
graphical detail).

Poem of My Cid

(Selections)

Poema de Mio Cid

(Selección)

[Tiradas 1–10 (versos 1–190):]
1. De los sos ojos tan fuertemientre llorando,
tornava la cabeça i estávalos catando.
Vío puertas abiertas e uços sin cañados,
alcándaras vázias sin pielles e sin mantos
e sin falcones e sin adtores mudados.
Sospiró mio Çid, ca mucho avié grandes cuidados.
Fabló mio Çid bien e tan mesurado:
"¡grado a tí, señor padre, que estás en alto!
"Esto me an buolto mios enemigos malos."
2. Allí pienssan de aguijar, allí sueltan las riendas.
Ala exida de Bivar ovieron la corneja diestra,
e entrando a Burgos oviéronla siniestra.
Meçió mio Çid los ombros y engrameó la tiesta:
"¡albricia, Alvar Fáñez, ca echados somos de tierra!
"*mas a grand ondra tornaremos a Castiella*".
3. Mio Çid Roy Díaz por Burgos entróve,
En sue conpaña sessaenta pendones;
exién lo veer mugieres e varones,
burgeses e burgesas, por las finiestras sone,
plorando de los ojos, tanto avién el dolore.
De las sus bocas todos dizían una razóne:
"¡Dios, qué buen vassallo, si oviesse buen señore!"
4. Conbidar le ien de grado, mas ninguno non osava:
el rey don Alfonsso tanto avié le grand saña.
Antes de la noche en Burgos dél entró su carta,
con grand recabdo e fuertemientre seellada:
que a mio Çid Roy Díaz que nadi nol diessen posada,

[Strophes 1–10 (verses 1–190):][1]

1. With tears streaming down his face,
he looked back and kept gazing at them.
He saw open entrances and doors without locks,
empty perches without pelisses or coverings,
without falcons, without goshawks that had already moulted.
My Cid sighed, for he had very great worries.
My Cid spoke, well and most prudently:
"My thanks to you, Lord and Father in heaven!
This was contrived for me by my bitter enemies."
2. Then they made ready to ride out, giving their steeds free rein.
As they departed from Vivar, the crow[2] was on their right;
as they entered Burgos, it was on their left.
My Cid shrugged his shoulders and shook his head:
"Good news, Álvar Fáñez, for we are exiled!
But we shall return to Castile in great honor."
3. My Cid Ruy Díaz entered Burgos,
with sixty mounted followers;
women and men left their houses to see him,
townsfolk male and female, and looked out their windows,
tears in their eyes because of their deep sorrow.
On their lips they all had the same words:
"God, what a good vassal, if only he had a good overlord!"
4. They would gladly have asked him in, but no one dared to:
so great was King Alfonso's rage against him.
The king's decree had reached Burgos the night before,
with many precautions,[3] heavily sealed:
no one was to offer lodgings to My Cid Ruy Díaz,

---

1. Since the first MS folio (which could have contained 50 verses) is missing, and the
-los ("them") in verse 2 seems to demand an antecedent (the Cid's retainers or his
buildings), most editors assume that the poem began with an announcement of the
Cid's exile, and possibly the reasons for it; elaborate reconstructions have been pro-
posed.   2. Or: "scops owl."   3. Or: "with harsh instructions."

3

e aquel que gela diesse sopiesse vera palabra
que perderié los averes e más los ojos de la cara,
e aun demás los cuerpos e las almas.
Grande duelo avién las yentes cristianas;
ascóndense de mio Çid, ca nol osan dezir nada.
El Campeador adeliñó a su posada;
así commo llegó á la puorta, fallóla bien çerrada,
por miedo del rey Alfons, que assí lo pararan:
que si non la quebrantás, que non gela abriessen por nada.
Los de mio Çid a altas vozes llaman,
los de dentro non les querién tornar palabra.
Aguijó mio Çid, a la puerta se llegaua,
sacó el pie del estribera, una ferídal dava;
non se abre la puerta, ca bien era çerrada.
Una niña de nuef años a ojo se parava:
"¡Ya Campeador, en buena çinxiestes espada!
"El rey lo ha vedado, anoch dél entró su carta,
"con grant recabdo e fuertemientre seellada.
"Non vos osariemos abrir nin coger por nada;
"si non, perderiemos los averes e las casas,
"e aun demás los ojos de las caras.
"Çid, en el nuestro mal vos non ganades nada;
"mas el Criador vos vala con todas sus vertudes santas."
Esto la niña dixo e tornós pora su casa.
Ya lo vede el Çid que del rey non avié graçia.
Partiós dela puerta, por Burgos aguijaua,
llegó a Santa María, luego descavalga;
fincó los inojos, de coraçón rogava.
La oración fecha, luego cavalgava;
salió por la puerta e Arlançón passava.
Cabo Burgos essa villa en la glera posava,
fincava la tienda e luego descavalgava.
Mio Çid Roy Díaz, el que en buena çinxo espada,
posó en la glera quando nol coge nadi en casa;
derredor dél una buena conpaña.
Assí posó mio Çid commo si fosse en montaña.
Vedada l'an conpra dentro en Burgos la casa
de todas cosas quantas son de vianda;
nol osarién vender al menos dinarada.

and anyone who did so might be assured
of losing his property and, what's more, the eyes in his head,
and furthermore his body and soul.
The Christian folk were greatly saddened;
they concealed themselves from My Cid, for they dared not speak a word to him.
The Battle Champion headed for his house;
on arriving at the door, he found it securely locked,
for fear of King Alfonso, for it had been so arranged:
unless he broke it down, they wouldn't let him in on any account.
My Cid's men shouted loudly,
those inside wouldn't make any reply.
My Cid spurred his horse and rode up to the door,
raised his foot from the stirrup, and gave it a kick;
the door didn't open, for it was securely locked.
A nine-year-old girl came into view:
"O Battle Champion, you that girded on your sword in a lucky hour!
The king has forbidden it, his decree arrived last night,
with many precautions, heavily sealed.
We wouldn't dare to let you in or welcome you on any account,
or else we'd lose our property and homes,
and furthermore the eyes in our heads.
Cid, from our misfortune you gain no advantage;
but may the Creator protect you with all his holy powers!"
This the girl said and went back home.
Now the Cid saw that the king hadn't pardoned him.
He left the doorway and rode swiftly through Burgos;
arriving at Santa María,[4] he dismounted at once;
he fell to his knees and prayed from his heart.
After praying he remounted;
he left the city gate and passed the Arlanzón.[5]
Outside the town of Burgos he camped on the gravel,
ordering his tent pitched and then dismounting.
My Cid Ruy Díaz, who girded on his sword in a lucky hour,
camped on the gravel since no one opened his home to him;
all around him was a numerous troop.
Thus My Cid camped as if in a wilderness.
Inside the town of Burgos he was forbidden to purchase
any of those things on which men subsist;
they wouldn't dare sell him even a farthing's worth.

---

4. The old cathedral.   5. The river to the east of Burgos.

5. Martín Antolínez, el Burgalés conplido,
a mio Çid e alos sos abástales de pan e de vino;
non lo conpra, ca él se lo avié consigo;
de todo conducho bien los ovo bastidos.
Pagós mio Çid el Campeador *conplido*
e todos los otros que van a so çervicio.
Fabló Martín Antolínez, odredes lo que a dicho:
"¡ya Canpeador, en buen ora fostes naçido!
"esta noch *y*agamos e vay*á*mosnos al matino,
"ca acusado seré de lo que vos he seruido,
"en ira del rey Alffons yo seré metido.
"Si con vusco escapo sano o bivo,
"aun çerca o tarde el rey querer m'a por amigo;
"si non, quanto dexo no lo preçio un figo."
6. Fabló mio Çid, el que en buen ora çinxo espada:
"Martin Antolínez, sodes ardida lança!
"si yo bivo, doblar vos he la soldada.
"Espeso e el oro e toda la plata,
"bien lo ve*e*des que yo no trayo *nada*,
"huebos me serié pora toda mi compaña;
"fer lo he amidos, de grado non avrié nada.
"Con vuestro consejo bastir quiero dos arcas;
"inchámoslas d'arena, ca bien serán pesadas,
"cubiertas de guadalmeçí e bien enclaveadas.
7. "Los guadameçís vermejos e los clavos bien dorados,
"Por Raquel e Vidas vayádesme privado:
"quando en Burgos me vedaron compra y el rey me a ayrado,
"non puedo traer el aver, ca mucho es pesado,
"enpeñar gelo he por lo que fore guisado;
"de noche lo lieven, que non lo vean cristianos.
"Véalo el Criador con todos los sos santos,
"yo más non puedo e amidos lo fago."
8. Martín Antolínez non lo detar*d*ava,
passó por Burgos, al castiello entrava,
por Raquel e Vidas apriessa demandava.
9. Raquel e Vidas en uno estavan amos,
en cuenta de sus averes, de los que avién ganados.
Llegó Martín Antolínez a guisa de menbrado:
"¿O sodes, Raquel e Vidas, los mios amigos caros?
"En poridad fablar querría con amos."
Non lo detardan, todos tres se apartaron.

5. Martín Antolínez, that excellent man of Burgos,
furnished My Cid and his men with bread and wine;
he didn't purchase it, for he already had a supply of it;
he fitted them out well with all sorts of provisions.
My Cid, the excellent Champion, was pleased,
as were all the others in his service.
Martín Antolínez spoke (you shall hear what he said):
"O Champion, you that were born in a lucky hour,
let us sleep here tonight and depart in the morning,
for I shall be blamed for assisting you,
and shall have incurred King Alfonso's official displeasure.
If I escape safe and sound along with you,
sooner or later the king will still cherish me as a friend;
if not, I don't give a fig for all that I leave behind."
6. My Cid spoke, he that girded on his sword in a lucky hour:
Martín Antolínez, you are a hardy warrior!
If I live, I shall double your pay.
I have spent all my gold and silver,
you can readily see that I possess nothing;
I need money for all my followers;
What I do will be done unwillingly, for nothing will be given to me voluntarily.
If you agree, I want to prepare two chests;
let us fill them with sand so they are very heavy,
cover them with embossed leather, and stud them with many nails.
7. The leather shall be red, and the studs well gilded.
Go swiftly, I pray you, to Raguel and Vidas:
say I am forbidden to make purchases in Burgos and am in disfavor with the king,
I cannot take away what I own, it weighs too much,
and I must pledge it for a reasonable amount;
let them carry it away at night, when not a Christian will see.
Let the Creator and all his saints witness it:
I am at the end of my tether, and I do this unwillingly."
8. Martín Antolínez made no delay,
he rode through Burgos, entered the citadel,
and urgently asked for Raguel and Vidas.
9. Raguel and Vidas were together,
reckoning up their profits.
Martín Antolínez arrived, acting shrewdly:
"Where are you, Raguel and Vidas, my dear friends?
I'd like to speak to both of you in secrecy."
Without delay all three withdrew to a private place.

"Raquel e Vidas, amos me dat las manos,
"que non me descubrades a moros nin a cristianos;
"por siempre vos faré ricos, que non seades menguados.
"El Campeador por las parias fo entrado,
"grandes averes priso e mucho sobejanos,
"retovo dellos quanto que fo algo;
"por en vino a aquesto por que fo acusado.
"Tiene dos arcas llennas de oro esmerado.
"Ya lo veedes que el rey le a ayrado.
"Dexado ha heredades e casas e palaçios.
"Aquellas non las puede levar, sinon, serié ventado;
"el Campeador dexar las ha en vuestra mano,
"e prestalde de aver lo que sea guisado.
"Prended las arcas e metedlas en vuestro salvo;
"con grand jura meted i las fedes amos,
"que non las catedes en todo aqueste año."
Raquel e Vidas seiense consejando:
"Nos huebos avemos en todo de ganar algo.
"Bien lo sabemos que él algo a gañado,
"quando a tierra de moros entró, que grant aver a sacado;
"non duerme sin sospecha qui aver trae monedado.
"Estas arcas prendámoslas amos,
"en logar las metamos que non sea ventado.
"Mas dezidnos del Çid, ¿de qué será pagado,
"o qué ganançia nos dará por todo aqueste año?"
Repuso Martín Antolínez a guisa de menbrado:
"myo Çid querrá lo que ssea aguisado;
"pedir vos a poco por dexar so aver en salvo.
"Acógensele omnes de todas partes menguados,
"a menester seysçientos marcos."
Dixo Raquel e Vidas: "dar gelos hemos de grado."
—"Ya vedes que entra la noch, el Çid es pressurado,
"huebos avemos que nos dedes los marcos."
Dixo Raquel e Vidas: "non se faze assí el mercado,
"sinon primero prendiendo e después dando."
Dixo Martín Antolínez: "yo desso me pago.
"Amos tred al Campeador contado,
"e nos vos ayudaremos, que assí es aguisado,
"por aduzir las arcas e meterlas en vuestro salvo,

"Raguel and Vidas, give me your hands, both of you,
as a token that you won't give me away to Moors or Christians;
I will make you rich forever, so that you never suffer any need.
The Champion entered Moorish territory to collect tribute;
he received great, truly outstanding treasures,
and kept for himself all that was most valuable in them;
for that reason he has incurred this blame.
He has two chests full of pure gold.
You can see that he has fallen into the king's disfavor.
He has abandoned his estates, houses, and ancestral home.
He cannot take away those chests, or else he'd be detected;
the Champion must leave them in your hands,
for which you will lend him a reasonable amount.
Take the chests and store them in safekeeping;
both of you, swear a strong oath and promise
not to inspect them for a whole year."
Raguel and Vidas conferred together:
"In every transaction we need to make a profit.
We're well aware that he gained a substantial sum
when he journeyed to Moorish lands, and brought back much property;
a man who bears coined wealth doesn't have a restful sleep.
Let the two of us take those chests,
and store them so secretly that no one will detect anything.
—But tell us about the Cid, what would he like to receive,
and what interest will he pay us for the yearlong loan?"
Martín Antolínez replied like a shrewd man:
"My Cid will request only what's reasonable;
he will ask you very little for leaving his money in safety.
Needy men from everywhere are joining his ranks,
so he needs six hundred marks."[6]
Raguel and Vidas said: "We'll gladly give it to him."
"You see that night is falling, the Cid is in a hurry,
we need to have you give us the marks."
Raguel and Vidas said: "That's not the way the transaction works;
rather, we must take first and give later."
Martín Antolínez said: "That suits me.
You two go to the renowned Champion,
and we will help you, as is only reasonable,
to bring the chests here and put them in your storage,

6. The mark was a unit of weight (8 ounces) for gold or silver.

"que non lo sepan moros nin cristianos."
Dixo Raquel e Vidas: "nos desto nos pagamos.
"Las archas aduchas, prendet seyesçientos marcos."
Martín Antolínez caualgó privado
con Raquel e Vidas, de voluntad e de grado.
Non viene a la puent, ca por el agua a passado,
que gelo non ventassen de Burgos omne nado.
Afévoslos a la tienda del Campeador contado;
assí commo entraron, al Çid besáronle las manos.
Sonrrisós mio Çid, estávalos fablando:
"¡ya don Raquel e Vidas, avédesme olbidado!
"Ya me exco de tierra, ca del rey so ayrado.
"A lo quem semeja, de lo mio avredes algo;
"mientra que vivades non seredes menguados."
Raquel e Vidas a mio Çid besáronle las manos.
Martín Antolínez el pleyto a parado,
que sobre aquellas arcas dar le ien seysçientos marcos,
e bien gelas guardarién fasta cabo del año;
ca assil dieran la fe*d* e gelo auién jurado,
que si antes las catassen que *f*ossen perjurados,
non les diesse mio Çid de ganancia un dinero malo.
Dixo Martín Antolínez: "carguen las arcas privado.
"Levaldas, Raquel e Vidas, ponedlas en vuestro salvo;
"yo iré convus*c*o, que adugamos los marcos,
"ca a mover *ha* mio Çid ante que cante el gallo."
Al cargar de las arcas veriedes gozo tanto:
non las podién poner en somo maguer eran esforçados.
Grádanse Raquel e Vidas con averes monedados,
ca mientras que visquiessen refechos eran amos.
10. Raquel a mio Çid la mano*l* *h*a besad*a*:
"¡Ya Canpeador, en buen*a* çinxiestes espada!
"de Castiella vos ides para las yentes estrañas,
"Assí es vuestra ventura, grandes son vuestras ganancias;
"una piel vermeja morisca e ondrada,
"Çid, beso vuestra mano en don que la yo aya."
—"Plazme", dixo el Çid, "daquí sea mandada.
"Si vos la aduxier dallá; si non, contalda sobre las arcas."
Raquel e Vidas las arcas levavan,

without either Moors or Christians learning of it."
Raguel and Vidas said: "That suits us.
Once the chests have been brought here, you'll get six hundred marks."
Martín Antolínez rode swiftly
with Raguel and Vidas, glad and contented.
He didn't cross the bridge, he forded the river,
so that not a soul in Burgos would get wind of the matter.
Now they now were at the tent of the renowned Champion;
as soon as they entered, they kissed the Cid's hands.
My Cid smiled, and began to address them:
"O Don Raguel and Vidas, you have forgotten me!
I am leaving this land, for I am in disfavor with the king.
As it seems to me, you will come into some of my property;
as long as you live you will never be needy."
Raguel and Vidas kissed My Cid's hands.
Martín Antolínez drew up the contract,
stating that they'd give him six hundred marks with those chests as security,
and would keep them safely for him until a year had gone by;
for thus they had promised him, swearing an oath to him
that, if they inspected them before then, they'd be perjurors
and My Cid wouldn't give them a red cent in interest.
Martín Antolínez said: "Pick up the chests quickly.
Raguel and Vidas, take them and store them away;
I'll go with you so we can bring back the marks,
because My Cid must move out before cockcrow."
When they picked up the chests there was great amusement:[7]
they couldn't lift them, though they were robust men.
Raguel and Vidas were pleased by that coined wealth,
for the two of them were now rich for the rest of their lives.
10. Raguel kissed My Cid's hand:
"O Champion, you that girded on your sword in a lucky hour!
You are leaving Castile to journey among foreign folk.
Your good luck is such that you will make great gains;
an expensive Moorish red fur jacket—
Cid, I kiss your hand to request it as a gift from you."
"Very well," said the Cid, "consider it as promised from this moment on.
If I don't bring it back to you from there, deduct the value of it from the chests."[8]
Raguel and Vidas carried away the chests;

7. Or: "hubbub."   8. The next three lines are not in the MS, but were added to fill
in a perceived lacuna in the text. This is always the case when entire lines are italicized
in this Spanish text.

con ellos *Martín Antolínez por Burgos entrava.*
Con todo recabdo llegan a la posada;
en medio del palaçio tendieron un almoçalla,
sobrella una sávana de rançal e muy blanca.
A tod el primer colpe trezientos marcos de plata,
notólos don Martino, sin peso los tomava;
los otros trezientos en oro gelos pagavan.
Çinco escuderos tiene don Martino, a todos los cargava.
Quando esto ovo fecho, odredes lo que fablava:
"ya don Raquel e Vidas, en vuestras manos son las arcas;
"yo, que esto vos gané, bien mereçía calças."

[**Tiradas 14–17** (versos 232–294):]
14. Tornavas *don* Martino a Burgos e mio Çid aguijó
pora San Pero de Cardeña quanto pudo a espolón,
con estos cavalleros quel sirven a so sabor.
Apriessa cantan los gallos e quieren crebar albores,
quando llegó a San Pero el buen Campeador;
el abbat don Sancho, cristiano del Criador,
rezaba los matines abuelta de los albores.
Y estava doña Ximena con çinco dueñas de pro,
rogando a San Pero e al Criador:
"Tú que a todos guías, val a mio Çid el Campeador."
15. Llamavan a la puerta, i sopieron el mandado;
¡Dios, qué alegre fo el abbat don Sancho!
Con lumbres e con candelas al corral dieron salto,
con tan grant gozo reçiben al que en buen ora nasco.
"Gradéscolo a Dios, mio Çid", dixo el abbat don Sancho;
"pues que aquí vos veo, prendet de mí ospedado."
Dixo el Çid, *el que en buen ora nasco:*
"graçias, don abbat, e so vuestro pagado;
"yo adobaré conducho pora mí e pora mios vasallos;
"mas por que me vo de tierra, dovos çinquaenta marcos,
"si yo algún día visquiero, seervos han doblados.

with them Martín Antolínez entered Burgos.
With great caution they arrived at their lodgings;
in the middle of the main room they unfurled a bedspread,
and, over it, a gleaming-white linen sheet.
In a single movement, they poured out three hundred marks of silver;
Don Martín counted it, without bothering to weigh it;
the other three hundred they paid him in gold.
Don Martín had five pages, and he distributed the load among them.
After doing this, listen to what he said:
"O Don Raguel and Vidas, the chests are in your hands;
For bringing you this profit I surely have earned a pair of hose as commission."

[SUMMARY of strophes **11–13** (verses 191–231): The moneylenders give Martín thirty marks as commission. He brings the gold and silver to the Cid, and, the deadline for leaving Castile drawing near, the Cid heads for the monastery of San Pedro de Cardeña, where his wife and daughters have been staying, while Martín returns to Burgos to take leave of his own family. The Cid preys to the Virgin for good fortune.]

[**Strophes 14–17** (verses 232–294):]
14. Don Martín returned to Burgos, and My Cid hastened
to San Pedro de Cardeña as fast as he could spur,
along with those horsemen who served him gladly.
The roosters crowed with urgency, and dawn was about to break,
when the good Champion reached San Pedro;
the abbot Don Sancho, a true Christian lover of his Creator,
was chanting matins as day was breaking.
And Doña Jimena was there with five excellent ladies,
praying to Saint Peter and the Creator:
"You who guide all things, protect My Cid the Champion!"
15. A call came at the door and they learned the news of his arrival;
God, how happy the abbot Don Sancho was!
The monks rushed out to the courtyard with candles and tapers,
welcoming with great joy the man born in a lucky hour.
"I thank God, My Cid," said the abbot Don Sancho;
"since I see you here, let me offer you hospitality."
The Cid, he that was born in a lucky hour, said:
"Thanks, lord abbot, I am much obliged to you;
I shall prepare provisions for myself and my vassals;
but because I am going into exile, here are fifty marks;
if I live long enough, you will receive double that amount.

"Non quiero far en el monesterio un dinero de daño;
"evades aquí por doña Ximena dovos çient marcos;
"a ella e a sus fijas e a sus dueñas sirvádeslas est año.
"Dues fijas dexo niñas e prendetlas en los braços;
"aquí vos *las* acomiendo a vos, abbat don Sancho;
"dellas e de mi mugier fagades todo recabdo.
"Si essa despenssa vos falleçiere o vos menguare algo,
"bien las abastad, yo assí vos lo mando;
"por un marco que despendades al monesterio daré yo quatro."
Otorgado gelo avié el abbat de grado.
Afevos doña Ximena con sus fijas do va llegando;
señas dueñas las traen e adúzenlas *en los braços.*
Ant el Campeador doña Ximena fincó los inojos amos,
Llorava de los ojos, quísol besar las manos:
"¡Merced, Canpeador, en ora buena fostes nado!
"Por malos mestureros de tierra sodes echado.
16. "¡Merçed, ya Çid, barba tan complida!
"Fem ante vos yo e vuestras ffijas,
"iffantes son e de días chicas,
"con aquestas mis dueñas de quien so yo servida,
"Yo lo veo que estades vos en ida
"e nos de vos partir nos hemos en vida.
"¡Dandnos consejo por amor de santa María!"
Enclinó las manos la barba vellida,
a las sues fijas en braço' las prendía,
llególas al coraçón, ca mucho las quería.
Llora de los ojos, tan fuerte mientre sospira:
"¡Ya doña Ximena, la mi mugier tan complida,
"commo a la mie alma yo tanto vos quería.
"Ya lo veedes que partir nos emos en vida,
"yo iré y vos fincaredes remanida.
"Plega a Dios e a santa María,
"que aun con mis manos case estas mis fijas,
"e quede ventura y algunos días vida,
"e vos, mugier ondrada, de mí seades servida!"
17. Grand yantar le fazen al buen Canpeador.
Tañen las campanas en San Pero a clamor.
Por Castiella odiendo van los pregones,
commo se va de tierra mio Çid el Canpeador;

I don't want to cause the monastery a farthing's expense;
see: here are a hundred marks to take care of Doña Jimena;
for the year to come serve her, her daughters, and her ladies.
I leave behind two young daughters; take them in your arms;
I here entrust them to you, abbot Don Sancho;
take the best of care of them and my wife.
If this money should run out, or should you lack for anything,
provide well for them, those are my orders;
for every mark you spend in the monastery I'll repay you four."
The abbot was glad to grant his request.
Behold, Doña Jimena and her daughters approached;
each girl was carried over to him in a lady's arms.
Reaching the Champion, Doña Jimena fell on both knees.
She was shedding tears, she wished to kiss his hands:
"A favor, Champion, you that were born in a lucky hour!
You are going into exile because of evil-minded troublemakers.
16. A favor, O Cid, bearded warrior of great excellence!
See me and your daughters before you
(they are very young and of few years),
together with these ladies of mine who serve me.
I see that you are about to depart
and that we must be separated from you while still alive.
Give us counsel, for the love of the Blessed Virgin!"
He of the elegant beard stretched out his hands,
taking his daughters in his arms
and hugging them to his heart, for he loved them dearly.
He shed tears and sighed deeply:
"O Doña Jimena, my excellent wife,
I love you as much as my own soul.
As you see, we must be separated while still alive;
I shall depart, while you remain behind.
May it please God and the Blessed Virgin
that some day I may personally give these daughters of mine in marriage,
that good fortune and life may last for some time to come,[9]
and that you, my honored wife, may be served by me!"
17. They gave the good Champion a great banquet.
They rang the bells in San Pedro noisily.
Throughout Castile the heralds were heard
proclaiming the exile of My Cid the Champion;

9. Or, reading *que dé* instead of *quede:* "and that he [God] may give good fortune and life for some time to come." (Even further emendations have been suggested.)

unos dexan casas e otros onores.
En aqués día a la puent de Arlançón
çiento quinze cavalleros todos juntados son;
todos demandan por mio Çid el Campeador;
Martín Antolínez con ellos' cojó.
Vansse pora San Pero do está el que en buena naçió.

[**Tiradas 28–31** (versos 564–622):]
28. Por todas essas tierras ivan los mandados,
que el Campeador mio Çid allí avié poblado,
venido es a moros, exido es de cristianos;
en la su vezindad non se treven ganar tanto.
Alegrando se va mio Çid con todos sos vassallos;
el castiello de Alcoçer en paria va entrando.
29. Los de Alcoçer a mio Çid yal dan parias
e los de Teca e los de Terrer la casa;
a los de Calatauth, sabet, ma'les pesava.
Allí yogo mio Çid complidas quinze sedmanas.
Quando vido mio Çid que Alcoçer non se le dava,
elle fizo un art e non lo detardava:

some of his men left their ancestral homes; others, the lands they held from the king.
On that day at the bridge over the Arlanzón
a hundred fifteen horsemen were assembled;
they were all asking for My Cid the Champion;
Martín Antolínez joined them.
They headed for San Pedro to find the man born in a lucky hour.

[SUMMARY of strophes **18–27** (verses 295–563): The Cid tells his men he hopes to give them twice what they may be losing. They all attend matins at San Pedro, where Jimena utters a long prayer, with many references to biblical heroes whom God "delivered." The Cid tears himself away from his family "like a fingernail torn from the flesh." As the Cid continues southeastward, crossing the Duero, many others join his ranks. Appearing to him in a dream, the archangel Gabriel promises him success. On the exile-deadline day he has 300 horsemen and many foot soldiers. They cross the mountainous border between Castile and Moorish territory. While some of his men raid far afield, the Cid takes the town of Castejón de Henares by means of an ambush. Álvar Fáñez, leader of the lucrative raid, refuses the Cid's offer of a fifth of the spoils: he's waiting for bigger things. Unwilling to be burdened with livestock and captives in case Alfonso attacks, the Cid sells his own share to the Moors. Unable to hold onto Castejón for various reasons, he abandons it in good condition, and the Moors bless him. Living off the land, he proceeds northeastward in the direction of Zaragoza (Saragossa) until reaching the (fictitious??) town of Alcocer, which he determines to take. With a good supply of water, he builds a strong camp encircled by a trench.]

[**Strophes 28–31** (verses 564–622):]

28. Through that whole territory the news spread
that the Champion, My Cid, had settled there;
he had left Christian lands and had come among the Moors;
with him nearby, they were afraid to till and pasture as usual.
My Cid and all his vassals were of good cheer;
the fortress of Alcocer was beginning to pay tribute.
29. The inhabitants of Alcocer were now paying tribute to My Cid,
along with those of Ateca and the town of Terrer;
it grieved those of Calatayud, I'll have you know.
My Cid remained there for fifteen full weeks.
When My Cid saw that Alcocer wouldn't surrender to him,
he contrived a stratagem, which he set in motion without delay:

dexa una tienda fita e las otras levava,
cojó' Salón ayuso, la su seña alçada,
las lorigas vestidas e çintas las espadas,
a guisa de menbrado, por sacarlos a çelada.
Vidienlo los de Alcoçer, ¡Dios, cómmo se alabavan!
"Fallido *h*a a mio Çid el pan e la çevada.
"Las otras abés lieva, una tienda a dexada.
"De guisa va mio Çid commo si escapasse de arrancada;
"demos salto a él e feremos grant ganançia,
"antes quel prendan los de Ter*r*er *la casa,*
"*ca si ellos le prenden,* non nos darán dent nada;
"la paria qu' él a presa tornar nos la ha doblada."
Salieron de Alcoçer a una priessa much estraña.
Mio Çid, quando los vio fuera, cogiós commo de arrancada;
Cojós Salón ayuso con los sos abuelta *anda.*
Dizen los de Alcoçer: "¡ya se nos va la ganançia!"
Los grandes e los chicos fuera salto da*v*an,
al sabor del prender de lo al non pienssan nada,
abiertas dexan las puertas que ninguno non las guarda.
El buen Campeador la su cara tornava,
vío que entrellos y el castiello mucho avié grant plaça;
mandó tornar la seña, a priessa espoloneavan.
"¡Firidlos, cavalleros, todos sines dubdança:
"con la merçed del Criador nuestra es la ganançia!"
Bueltos son con ellos por medio de la llaña.
¡Dios, qué bueno es el gozo por aquesta mañana!
Mio Çid e Álbar Fáñez adelant aguijavan;
tienen buenos cavallos, sabet, a su guisa les andan;
entrellos y el castiello en essora entravan.
Los vassallos de mio Çid sin piedad les davan,
en un poco de logar trezientos moros matan.
Dando grandes alaridos los que están en la çelada,
dexando van los delant, por*a*l castiello se tornavan,
las espadas desnudas, a la puerta se paravan.
Luego llegavan los sos, ca fecha es el arrancada.
Mio Çid gañó a Alcoçer, sabet, por esta maña.
30. Vino Per Vermu*doz,* que la seña tiene en mano,
metióla en somo en todo lo mas alto.
Fabló mio Çid R*oy* Díaz, el que en buen ora fue nado:
"grado a Dios del çielo e a todos los sos santos,
"ya mejoraremos posadas a dueños e a cauallos.

leaving one tent standing, he struck the rest
and proceeded downstream along the Jalón—his banner raised,
his men wearing their coats of mail and their swords—
like a shrewd man, to lead the Moors into a trap.
The inhabitants of Alcocer, seeing this, were mightily pleased!
"My Cid has run out of bread for his men and feed for his horses.
Removing the other tents with difficulty, he has left behind only one.
My Cid is hastening as if escaping defeat;
let us sally out after him and win rich booty
before those of the town of Terrer seize it,
for if they do they won't give us any of it;
we will recover, twice over, the tribute he has taken."
They sallied out of Alcocer at extraordinary speed.
When My Cid saw them outside, he retreated as if from a defeat;
he proceeded downstream along the Jalón together with his men.
Those of Alcocer said: "Now the booty is getting away from us!"
One and all sallied out,
so eager to seize booty that they disregarded all else,
and leaving the town gates open with no one to guard them.
The good Champion looked back
and saw that there was a lot of space between them and the fortress;
he ordered his banner to face about, and his men spurred on swiftly.
"Strike them, horsemen, all of you fearlessly;
if the Creator favors us, the gain is ours!"
The two groups clashed in the middle of the plain.
God, how great was the joy that morning!
My Cid and Álvar Fáñez dashed ahead;
they had good steeds, I'll have you know, which obeyed them perfectly;
at that moment they arrived between the Moors and the fortress.
My Cid's vassals attacked them without mercy,
killing three hundred Moors in a brief space of time.
While those caught in the trap shrieked loudly,
the Cid's vanguard left the scene, hastened toward the fortress,
their swords bared, and arrived at the gate.
Then the rest of his men joined them, and the victory was won.
My Cid, I'll have you know, took Alcocer by means of that ruse.
30. Pedro Bermúdez rode up, the banner in his hand,
and he planted it on the loftiest place.
My Cid Ruy Díaz, he that was born in a lucky hour, said:
"I thank God in heaven and all his saints.
Now we shall have better lodgings for man and beast.

31. "¡Oíd a mí, Álbar Fáñez e todos los cavalleros!
"En este castiello grand aver avemos preso;
"los moros yazen muertos, de bivos pocos veo.
"Los moros e las moras vender non los podremos,
"que los descabeçemos nada non ganaremos;
"cojámoslos de dentro, ca el señorío tenemos;
"posaremos en sus casas e dellos nos serviremos."

[**Tiradas 33–36** (versos 656–732):]

33. Fincaron las tiendas e prendend las posadas,
creçen estos virtos, ca yentes son sobejanas.
Las arrobdas, que los moros sacan,
de día e de noch enbueltos andan en armas;
muchas son las arrobdas e grande es el almofalla.
A los de mio Çid ya les tuellen el agua.
Mesnadas de mio Çid exir querién a batalla,
el que en buen ora nasco firme gelo vedava.
Toviérongela en çerca complidas tres sedmanas.

34. A cabo de tres sedmanas, la quarta querié entrar,
mio Çid con los sos tornós a acordar:
"el agua nos an vedada, exir nos ha el pan,
"que nos queramos ir de noch no nos lo consintrán;
"grandes son los poderes por con ellos lidiar,
"dezidme, cavalleros, cómmo vos plaze de far."
Primero fabló Minaya, un cavallero de prestar:
"de Castiella la gentil exidos somos acá,
"si con moros non lidiáremos, no nos darán del pan.
"Bien somos nos seysçientos, algunos ay de más;
"en el nombre del Criador, que non passe por al:
"vayámoslos ferir en aquel día de cras."
Dixo el Campeador: "a mi guisa fablastes;
"ondrástesvos, Minaya, ca aver vos lo iedes de far."
Todos los moros e las moras de fuera los manda echar,

31. Hear me, Álvar Fáñez and all my horsemen!
In this fortress we have won rich spoils;
the Moors are dead, I see few still alive.
We won't be able to sell the Moorish men and women;
we have nothing to gain by cutting off their heads;
let's receive them into the town, since we are masters of it;
we'll dwell in their houses and use them as servants."

[SUMMARY of strophe **32** (verses 623–655): The Moors of Ateca, Terrer, and Calatayud inform the emir of Valencia of recent events. He sends three thousand horsemen to join local border troops and take the Cid alive. The massed forces, led by generals Fáriz and Galve, prepare to lay siege to Alcocer.]

[**Strophes 33–36** (verses 656–732):]

33. They pitched their tents and took up lodgings;
their forces grew, for they were populous nations.
The patrols sent out by the Moors
kept their armor on both day and night;
there were many patrols, and the main army was large.
Now they were cutting off My Cid's water supply.
My Cid's troops wanted to sally out and fight,
but the man born in a lucky hour forbade it strictly.
The Moors besieged his town for three full weeks.
34. At the end of three weeks, as the fourth was beginning,
My Cid held a conference with his men:
"They have cut off our water, our bread will soon run out;
if we wanted to leave at night, they wouldn't let us;
their forces are strong ones to meet in pitched battle;
tell me, knights, what you suggest we do."
The first to speak was Minaya,[10] an excellent knight:
"We have come this far in exile from fair Castile;
if we don't fight the Moors, they won't give us bread.
There are six hundred of us, and a little more;
in the name of the Creator, let it not be otherwise:
let's go and smite them tomorrow!"
The Champion said: "You have spoken to my mind;
you have done yourself honor, Minaya, just as I expected you to."
He ordered all the Moors, male and female, to be expelled from town

---

10. Álvar Fáñez.

que non sopiesse ninguno esta su poridad.
El día e la noche piénssanse de adobar.
Otro día mañana, el sol querié apuntar,
armado es mio Çid con quantos que él ha;
fablava mio Çid commo odredes contar:
"todos iscamos fuera, que nadi non raste,
"sinon dos pedones solos por la puerta guardar;
"si nos muriéremos en campo, en castiello nos entrarán,
"si vençiéremos la batalla, creçremos en rictad.
"E vos, Per Vermudoz, la mi seña tomad;
"commo sodes muy bueno, tener la edes sin arth;
"mas non aguijedes con ella, si yo non vos lo mandar."
Al Çid besó la mano, la seña va tomar.
Abrieron las puertas, fuera un salto dan;
viéronlo las arrobdas de los moros, al almofalla se van tornar.
¡Qué priessa va en los moros! e tornáronse a armar;
ante roído de atamores la tierra querié quebrar;
veriedes armarse moros, apriessa entrar en az.
De parte de los moros dos señas ha cabdales,
e los pendones mezclados, ¿qui los podrié contar?
Las azes de los moros yas mueven adelant,
por a mio Çid e a los sos a manos los tomar.
"Quedas seed, mesnadas, aquí en este logar,
"non derranche ninguno fata que yo lo mande."
Aquel Per Vermudoz non lo pudo endurar,
la seña tiene en mano, conpeçó de espolonar:
"¡El Criador vos vala, Çid Campeador leal!
"Vo meter la vuestra seña en aquella mayor az;
"los que el debdo avedes veré commo la acorrades."
Dixo el Campeador: "¡non sea, por caridad!"
Repuso Per Vermudoz: "non rastará por al."
Espolonó el cavallo, e metiól en el mayor az.
Moros le reçiben por la seña ganar,
danle grandes colpes, mas nol pueden falssar.
Dixo el Campeador: "¡valelde, por caridad!"
35. Enbraçan los escudos delant los coraçones,
abaxan las lanças abueltas de los pendones,
enclinaron las caras de suso de los arzones,

so that no one might learn his secret plan.
That day and night they were busy preparing their equipment.
The following morning, when the sun was about to appear,
My Cid and all his men were in armor;
My Cid spoke as you shall hear tell:
"Let us all issue forth, let no one remain behind
except for two foot soldiers to guard the town gate;
if we die in battle, they will enter our fortress;
if we win the fight, our wealth will increase.
And you, Pedro Bermúdez, take up my standard;
since you are a fine soldier, you will bear it loyally;
but don't ride out ahead with it unless I order you to."
He kissed the Cid's hand and he took up the standard.
They opened the gates and sallied out;
they were seen by the Moorish scouts, who returned to their army.
What an alarm among the Moors, who began putting on their armor!
Their drums made such a racket, the ground nearly split;
there you might see Moors arming and hastening into formation.
On the Moors' side there were two generals' standards
and, as for the various pennants,[11] who could count them?
The Moorish files were now moving forward,
to come to grips with My Cid and his men.
"Men, stand pat right here;
no one is to break ranks until I give the order."
But Pedro Bermúdez was unable to sit tight;
the standard in his hand, he began to spur forward:
"May the Creator protect you, loyal Champion Cid!
I shall plant your standard amid that larger group;[12]
I'll see how all you sworn vassals come to its aid."
The Champion said: "I beg you not to!"
Pedro Bermúdez replied: "It can't be any other way!"
He spurred his horse, and planted it amid the larger group.
The Moors let him through so they could capture the standard;
they struck him mighty blows, but couldn't pierce his armor.
The Champion said: "For God's sake, help him!"
35. They gripped their shields and covered their hearts,
they lowered their pennanted lances,
bent their faces over their saddletrees,

---

11. The MS reads *peones mezclados* ("foot soldiers from different areas"), which many editors accept.   12. Assuming that the Moorish army was tactically divided in two. Perhaps: "amid the thick of their troops."

ívanlos ferir de fuertes coraçones.
A grandes vozes llama el que en buen ora naçió:
"¡feridlos, cavalleros, por amor del *Criador!*
"¡Yo so Roy Díaz, el Çid de Bivar Campeador!"
Todos fieren en el az do está Per Vermudoz.
Trezientas lanças son, todas tienen pendones;
seños moros mataron, todos de seños colpes;
a la tornada que fazen otros tantos *muertos* son.
36. Veriedes tantas lanças premer e alçar,
tanta adágara foradar e passar,
tanta loriga falssar *e* desmanchar,
tantos pendones blancos salir vermejos en sangre,
tantos buenos cavallos sin sos dueños andar.
Los moros llaman Mafómat e los cristianos santi Yague.
Cadién *por el campo* en un poco de logar
moros muertos mill e trezientos ya.

[**Tiradas 38–41** (versos 744–825):]
38. A Minaya Álbar Fáñez matáronle el cavallo,
bien lo acorren mesnadas de cristianos.
La lança a quebrada, al espada metió mano,
maguer de pie buenos colpes va dando.
Víolo mio Çid Roy Díaz el Castellano,
acostós a un aguazil que tenié buen cavallo,
diol tal espadada con el so diestro braço,
cortól por la çintura, el medio echó en campo.
A Minaya Álbar Fáñez ival dar el cavallo:
"¡Cavalgad, Minaya, vos sodes el mio diestro braço!
"Oy en este día de vos abré grand bando;
"firme' son los moros, aun nos' van del campo,
"*a menester que los cometamos de cabo.*"
Cavalgó Minaya, el espada en la mano,
por estas fuerças fuerte mientre lidiando,
a los que alcança valos delibrando.
Mio Çid Roy Díaz, el que en buena nasco,
al rey Fáriz tres colpes le avié dado;
los dos le fallen, y el únol ha tomado,
por la loriga ayuso la sangre destellando;

and rode out to battle with brave hearts.
He that was born in a lucky hour exclaimed loudly:
"Strike them, horsemen, for the love of the Creator!
I am Ruy Díaz, the Cid and Champion of Vivar!"
They all attacked the section where Pedro Bermúdez was.
They were three hundred lancers, each lance with a pennant;
they slew three hundred Moors, each at one blow,
and killed an equal number on their second charge.
36. How many lances could be seen lowered and raised,
how many leather shields pierced and penetrated,
how many coats of mail perforated and ripped open,
how many white pennants reddened with blood,
how many fine horses running about riderless!
The Moors called on Mohammed, and the Christians on Saint James.
In a brief space of time there had already fallen in the field
one thousand three hundred slain Moors.

[SUMMARY of strophe 37 (verses 733–743): The names of the Christian leaders.]

[Strophes 38–41 (verses 744–825):]
38. Minaya Álvar Fáñez had his horse killed under him,
but troops of Christians hastened to his aid.
His lance broken, he seized his sword
and, though on foot, dealt hefty blows.
My Cid Ruy Díaz of Castile saw him,
rode up to a vizier who had a good horse,
and gave him such a mighty right-handed sword stroke
that he severed him at the waist, his upper body falling to the ground.
He hastened to give the horse to Minaya Álvar Fáñez:
"Ride, Minaya, you that are my right arm!
This day I shall receive much aid from you;
the Moors are steadfast, they still aren't quitting the field;
we must attack them head on."
Minaya rode, sword in hand,
through those forces, fighting bravely,
dispatching all he came across.
My Cid Ruy Díaz, he that was born in a lucky hour,
had given General Fáriz three blows;
two missed, but one of them hit its mark,
making his blood flow down his coat of mail;

bolvió la rienda por írsele del campo.
Por aquel colpe rancado es el fonssado.
39. Martín Antolínez un colpe dio a Galve,
las carbonclas del yelmo echógelas aparte,
cortól el yelmo, que llegó a la carne;
sabet, el otro non gel osó esperar.
Arrancado es el rey Fáriz e Galve;
¡tan buen día por la cristiandad,
ca fuyen los moros della *e della* part!
Los de mio Çid firiendo en alcaz,
el rey Fáriz en Ter*r*er se *f*o entrar,
e a Galve nol cogieron allá;
para Calatayu*t*h quanto puede se va.
El Campeador íval en alcaz,
fatal Calatayu*t*h duró el segudar.
40. A Mynaya Álbar Fáñez bien l'anda el cavallo,
daquestos moros mató treínta e quatro;
espada tajador, sangriento trae el braço,
por el cobdo ayuso la sangre destellando.
Dize Minaya: "agora so pagado,
"que a Castiella irán buenos mandados,
"que mio Çid R*o*y Díaz lid campal a *arrancado.*"
Tantos moros yazen muertos que pocos bivos a dexados,
ca en alcaz sin dubda les *f*oron dando.
Yas tornan los del que en buen ora nasco.
Andava mio Çid sobre so buen cavallo,
la cofia fronzida ¡Dios, cómmo es bien barbado!
almófar a cuestas, la espada en la mano.
Vio los sos commos van allegando:
"Grado a Dios, aquel que está en alto,
"quando tal batalla avemos arrancado."
Esta albergada los de mio Çid luego la an robad*o*
de escudos e de armas e de otros averes largos;
de los moriscos, quando son llegados,
ffallaron quinientos e diez cavallos.
Grand alegreya va entre essos cristianos,
más de quinze de los sos menos non fallaron.
Traen oro e plata que non saben recabdo;
refechos son todos essos cristianos
con aquesta ganançia *que y avién fallado.*
A so castiello a los moros dentro los an tornados,

he turned his horse to ride off the field.
By that blow his army was conquered.
39. Martín Antolínez gave Galve a blow
which loosened the garnets on his helmet
and cut through the helmet, reaching the flesh;
I'll have you know he didn't dare wait for the second blow.
Generals Fáriz and Galve were defeated;
what a joyous day for Christianity,
with the Moors fleeing in every direction!
With My Cid's men in hot pursuit,
General Fáriz gained admittance into Terrer,
but Galve found no asylum there;
he proceeded toward Calatayud as fast as he could go.
The Champion rode after him,
the chase lasting all the way to Calatayud.
40. Minaya Álvar Fáñez's horse was a good one,
and he killed thirty-four of those Moors;
his sword a biting one, his arm was covered with blood,
which streamed down his elbow.
Minaya said: "Now I'm contented,
because the good news will reach Castile
that My Cid Ruy Díaz has won a pitched battle."
So many Moors lay dead that very few were left alive,
for they were pursuing and smiting them fearlessly.
Now they returned, the followers of the man born in a lucky hour.
My Cid was riding his noble steed,
his cloth cap wrinkled (Lord, how fine his beard was!),
his hood of mail hanging over his shoulders, his sword in his hand.
He saw his men approaching him:
"I thank God on high
because we have won so great a battle."
Then My Cid's men despoiled that camp
of shields, weapons, and numerous other goods;
when the Moorish horses were rounded up,
they numbered five hundred ten.
There was great good cheer among those Christians,
for they hadn't lost more than fifteen men.
They gained more gold and silver than they could reckon up;
all those Christians were made rich
by the booty they had found there.
They let the Moors back into their fortress,

mandó mio Çid aun que les diessen algo.
Grant a el gozo mio Çid con todos sos vassallos.
Dio a partir estos dineros e estos averes largos;
en la su quinta al Çid caen cient cavallos.
¡Dios, qué bien pagó a todos sus vassallos,
a los peones e a los encavalgados!
Bien lo aguisa el que en buen ora nasco,
quantos él trae todos son pagados.
"¡Oíd, Minaya, sodes mio diestro braço!
"D'aquesta riqueza que el Criador nos a dado
"a vuestra guisa prended con vuestra mano.
"Enbiar vos quiero a Castiella con mandado
"desta batalla que avemos arrancado;
"al rey Alfons que me a ayrado
"quiérol enbiar en don treínta cavallos,
"todos con siellas e muy bien enfrenados,
"señas espadas de los arzones colgando."
Dixo Minaya Álbar Fáñez: "esto faré yo de grado."
41. "—Evades aquí oro e plata *fina*,
"una uesa lleña, que nada nol mingua;
"en Santa María de Burgos quitedes mill missas:
"lo que romaneçiere daldo a mi mugier e a mis fijas,
"que rueguen por mí las noches e los días;
"si les yo visquier, serán dueñas ricas."

[**Tiradas 45–48** (versos 846–898):]
45. ¡Mio Çid Ruy Díaz a Alcoçer *ha* ven*d*ido;
qué bien pagó á *sos* vassallos mismos!
A cavalleros e a peones fechos los ha ricos,
en todos los sos non fallariedes un mesquino.
Qui a buen señor sirve, siempre bive en deliçio.
46. Quando mio Çid el castiello quiso quitar,
moros e moras tomáronse a quexar:
"¿vaste, mio Çid? ¡nuestras oraçiones váyante delante!
"Nos pagados finc*amos*, señor, de la tu part."

and My Cid even ordered that they should be given part of the proceeds.
My Cid and all his vassals were overjoyed.
He distributed the money and the extensive spoils;
as part of his own fifth the Cid gained a hundred horses.
Lord, how well he remunerated all his vassals,
both the foot soldiers and the cavalry!
He that was born in a lucky hour made a fair distribution,
and all his men were satisfied.
"Hear me, Minaya, you that are my right arm!
From this wealth which the Creator has given us
take as much as you like.
I want to send you to Castile with the news
of this battle which we have won;
to King Alfonso, who holds me in disfavor,
I wish to send as a gift thirty horses,
all with saddles and very good bits,
and with a sword attached to each saddletree."
Minaya Álvar Fáñez said: "I shall do that gladly."
41. "Here you see gold and fine silver,
a tall riding boot full, with no space to spare;
at Santa María in Burgos pay for a thousand masses:
whatever is left over, give to my wife and daughters,
so they may pray for me every night and day;
if I live, they will be wealthy women."

[SUMMARY of strophes **42–44** (verses 826–845): The Cid tells Álvar
Fáñez to seek him out wherever he may be upon returning from
Castile, because Alcocer might be too hard to hold onto. And, indeed,
the Cid sells the town to the nearby Moors for three thousand marks
of silver.]

[Strophes 45–48 (verses 846–898):]
45. My Cid Ruy Díaz has sold Alcocer;
how well he paid his own vassals!
He has enriched horsemen and foot soldiers;
among all his men you couldn't find a poor one.
The man who serves a good lord always lives in delight.
46. When My Cid was about to leave the fortress,
the Moors, male and female, began to lament:
"Are you going, My Cid? May our prayers precede you!
We are contented, master, with the way you have treated us."

Quando quitó a Alcoçer mio Çid el de Bivar,
moros e moras compeçaron de llorar.
Alçó su seña, el Campeador se va,
passó Salón ayuso, aguijó cabadelant,
al exir de Salón mucho ovo buenas aves.
Plogo a los de Terrer e a los de Calatayut más,
pesó a los de Alcocer, ca pro les fazié grant.
Aguijó mio Çid, ivas cabadelant,
y ffincó en un poyo que es sobre Mont Real;
alto es el poyo, maravilloso e grant;
non teme guerra, sabet, a nulla part.
Metió en paria a Daroca enantes,
desí a Molina, que es del otra part,
la terçera Teruel, que estava delant;
en su mano tenié a Çelfa la de Canal.
47. ¡Mio Çid Roy Díaz de Dios aya su graçia!
Ido es a Castiella Álbar Fáñez Minaya,
treynta cavalos al rey los enpresentava;
vídolos el rey, fermoso sonrrisava:
"¿quin los dio estos, si vos vala Dios, Minaya?"
"—Mio Çid Roy Díaz, que en buen ora cinxo espada.
"Pues quel vos ayrastes, Alcoçer gañó por maña;
"al rey de Valençia dello el mensaje llegava,
"mandólo y çercar, e tolléronle el agua.
"Mio Çid salió del castiello, en campo lidiava,
"venció dos reyes de moros en aquesta batalla,
"sobejana es, señor, la sue ganançia.
"A vos, rey ondrado, enbía esta presentaja;
"bésavos los piedes e las manos amas
"quel ayades merçed, si el Criador vos vala."
Dixo el rey: "mucho es mañana,
"omne ayrado, que de señor non ha graçia,
"por acogello a cabo de tres sedmanas.
"Mas después que de moros fo, prendo esta presentaja;
"aun me plaze de mio Çid que fizo tal ganançia.
"Sobresto todo, a vos quito, Minaya,
"honores e tierras avellas condonadas,
"id e venit, d'aquí vos do mi graçia;
"mas del Çid Campeador, yo non vos digo nada.
48. "Sobre aquesto todo, dezir vos quiero, *Álbar Fáñez:*
"de todo mio reyno los que lo quisieren far,

When My Cid, lord of Vivar, left Alcocer,
the Moors, male and female, started to weep.
He raised his banner, the Champion moved out;
he followed the Jalón downstream, proceeding straight ahead;
when he moved away from the Jalón there were very good omens.
The people of Terrer were pleased, those of Calatayud even more so,
but those of Alcocer were grieved, for he had benefited them greatly.
My Cid proceeded on his way, heading straight forward,
camping on the hill El Poyo overlooking Monreal del Campo;
the hill was high, wondrous and grand;
I'll have you know he had no fear of being attacked on any side.
Previously he had placed Daroca under tribute,
and also Molina de Aragón, which is in the opposite direction,
and thirdly Teruel, which is some distance from El Poyo;
he also held Cella in his power.
47. May My Cid Ruy Díaz enjoy God's grace!
Álvar Fáñez Minaya has arrived in Castile
and has made the king the present of thirty horses;
on seeing them, the king smiled pleasantly:
"Who has given these to me, Minaya (so may God keep you!)?"
"My Cid Ruy Díaz, who girded on his sword in a lucky hour.
After falling into your disfavor, he took Alcocer by a ruse;
news of this reached the emir of Valencia,
who ordered a siege, during which his water supply was cut off.
My Cid sallied out of the fortress and fought a pitched battle,
conquering two Moorish generals in that fight;
his spoils are remarkable, my liege.
To you, honored king, he sends this gift;
he kisses your feet and both your hands,
asking you to forgive him (so may the Creator keep you!)."
The king said: "It is far too soon
to welcome back a man out of favor with his lord
after only three weeks.
But, since it was Moorish property, I accept this present;
I am also pleased that My Cid won so much booty.
Furthermore, Minaya, I pardon you;
take back your awarded properties and family lands,
come and go freely; from this moment on I restore my favor to you;
but with regard to the Cid and Champion, I say nothing.
48. What's more, Álvar Fáñez, I wish to tell you:
throughout my kingdom, all who desire

"buenos e valientes pora mio Çid huyar,
"suéltoles los cuerpos e quítoles las heredades."
Besóle las manos Minaya Álbar Fáñez:
"Grado e graçias, rey, commo a señor natural;
"esto feches agora, al feredes adelant;
"con Dios nós guisaremos commo vós lo fagades."
Dixo el rey: "Minaya, esso sea de vagar.
"Id por Castiella e déxenvos andar,
"si'nulla dubda id a mio Çid buscar."

[**Tiradas 55–63** (versos 956–1084):]
55. Los mandados son idos a *las* partes todas;
llegaron las nuevas el comde de Barçilona,
que mio Çid Roy Díaz quel corrié la tierra toda;
ovo grand pesar e tóvoslo a grand fonta.
56. El conde es muy follón e dixo una vanidat:
"Grandes tuertos me tiene mio Çid el de Bivar.
"Dentro en mi cort tuerto me tovo grand:
"firióm el sobrino e non lo enmendó más;
"agora córrem las tierras que en mi enpara están;
"non lo desafié nil torné *el* amiztad,
"mas quando él me lo busca, ir gelo he yo demandar."
Grandes son los poderes e a priessa llegandos van,
entre moros e cristianos gentes se le allegan grandes,
adeliñan tras mio Çid el bueno de Bivar,
tres días e dos noches penssaron de andar,
alcançaron a mio Çid en Tévar e el pinar;
así vienen esforçados que a manos se le cuydan tomar.
Mio Çid don Rodrigo trae gananças grand,
diçe de una sierra e llegava a un val.
Del conde don Remont venido lês mensaje;

to aid My Cid as loyal, brave followers
may depart freely without the loss of their possessions."
Minaya Álvar Fáñez kissed his hands:
"I thank you, sire, as my feudal lord;
this you do today, in the future you will do more;
with God's help we'll act in such a way that you *shall*."
The king said: "Minaya, there is no hurry about that.
Travel through Castile and roam freely,
rejoin My Cid without any fear."

[SUMMARY of strophes **49–54** (verses 899–955): After 15 weeks of successful raiding from his base at El Poyo, the Cid moves eastward to Tévar; from there he even exacts tribute from Zaragoza. Three weeks after the move, he is joined by Álvar Fáñez and 200 new riders, plus more infantry. They raid the territory of Alcañiz (closer to Zaragoza), and other cities feel threatened as the Cid leaves Tévar and raids more extensively.]

[Strophes 55–63 (verses 956–1084):]

55. Messengers have traveled everywhere;
the news reached the count of Barcelona
that My Cid Ruy Díaz was overrunning his whole territory;
he was deeply grieved, considering it a serious insult.
56. The count, who was a great braggart, uttered vain words:
"My Cid, that fellow from Vivar, has offended me gravely.
Here in my court he did me a great wrong:
he struck my nephew[13] and never gave satisfaction for it;
now he's raiding lands that are under my protection;[14]
I haven't challenged him or declared war on him,
but since he's asking for it, I must exact redress from him."
Great were his forces, which gathered rapidly;
numerous men, both Moors and Christians, joined him,
and they set out after My Cid, the good lord of Vivar;
they kept on going for three days and two nights,
and came up with My Cid in the pinewoods of Tévar;
they were so enthusiastic that they expected to take him prisoner.
My Cid Don Rodrigo was carrying enormous booty;
he descended from a mountain range into a valley.
A message came to him from Count Ramón;

---

13. An otherwise unrecorded incident.   14. The small Moorish realm of Lérida.

mio Çid quando lo oyó, enbió pora allá:
"digades al conde non lo tenga a mal,
"de lo so non lievo nada, déxem ir en paz."
Respuso el comde: "¡esto non será verdad!
"Lo de antes e de agora tódom lo pechará;
"sabrá el salido a quien vino desondrar."
Tornós el mandadero quanto pudo más.
Essora la connosçe mio Çid el de Bivar
que a menos de batalla nos pueden den quitar.
57. "Ya cavalleros, apart fazed la ganançia;
"apriessa vos guarnid e metedos en las armas;
"el comde don Remont dar nos ha grant batalla,
"de moros e de cristianos gentes trae sobejanas,
"a menos de batalla non nos dexarié por nada.
"Pues adelant irán tras nos, aquí sea la batalla;
"apretad los cavallos, e bistades las armas.
"Ellos vienen cuesta yuso, e todos trahen calças;
"elas siellas coçeras e las cinchas amojadas;
"nos cavalgaremos siellas gallegas, e huesas sobre calças;
"ciento cavalleros devemos vençer aquellas mesnadas.
"Antes que ellos lleguen a llaño, presentémosles las lanças;
"por uno que firgades, tres siellas irán vázias.
"Verá Remont Verenguel tras quien vino en alcança
"oy en este pinar de Tévar por tollerme la ganançia."
58. Todos son adobados quando mio Çid esto ovo fablado;
las armas avién presas e sedién sobre los cavallos.
Vidieron la cuesta yuso la fuerça de los francos;
al fondón de la cuesta, çerca es de'llaño,
mandólos ferir mio Çid, el que en buen ora nasco;
esto fazen los sos de voluntad e de grado;
los pendones e las lanças tan bien las van enpleando,
a los unos firiendo e a los otros derrocando.
Vençido a esta batalla el que en buena nasco;
al comde don Remont a preson le a tomado;
hi gañó a Colada que más vale de mill marcos.
59. I venció esta batalla por o ondró su barba;
prísolo al comde, pora su tienda lo levava;
a sos creenderos guardar lo mandava.
De fuera de la tienda un salto dava,

when My Cid heard it, he sent back the reply:
"Tell the count not to hold it against me;
I'm not taking anything of his; he should let me go in peace."
The count retorted: "By no means!
He shall pay me for all he's done in the past and now;
the exile will find out whom he has come and dishonored!"
The herald returned as fast as he could.
Then My Cid, lord of Vivar, realized
that he couldn't get off without a battle.
57. "O horsemen, move the booty aside;
equip yourselves quickly and put on your armor;
Count Ramón will fight a great battle with us;
he brings numerous soldiers, Moors and Christians;
there is no way that he'll let us alone without fighting.
Since they will keep following us, let the battle be here;
tighten the girths on your horses, and put on your armor.
They are coming downhill, and they are all wearing fancy hose on their legs;
they have racing saddles with slack girths;
we will be riding on Galician saddles and wearing high boots over our hose;
we, being a hundred horsemen, must vanquish those large forces.
Before they reach level ground, let's have our lances ready;
with every blow you strike there will be three empty saddles.
Ramón Berenguer will see whom he has been pursuing
today in this pinewood of Tévar to rob me of my booty!"
58. When My Cid had finished this speech, everyone was ready;
they had taken their weapons and were sitting their mounts.
They saw the Catalan forces on the hillside;
at the foot of the hill, near the level ground,
My Cid, he that was born in a lucky hour, ordered them to charge;
his men did so readily and gladly;
they made very good use of their pennanted lances,
striking some and unhorsing others.
He that was born in a lucky hour won that battle;
he took Count Ramón prisoner;
there he won Colada,[15] which was worth over a thousand marks.
59. There he won that battle whereby he honored his beard.
He captured the count, taking him to his tent,
where he ordered his pesonal servants to guard him.
He dashed out of the tent,

---

15. One of the Cid's two famous swords.

de todas partes los sos se ajunta*van;*
plogo a mio Çid, ca grandes son las ganançias.
A mio Çid don Rodrigo grant cozínal adobavan;
el conde don Remont non gelo preçia nada;
adúzenle los comeres, delant gelos paravan,
él non lo quiere comer, a todos los sosañava:
"Non combré un bocado por quanto ha en toda España,
"antes perderé el cuerpo e dexaré el alma,
"pues que tales malcalçados me vençieron de batalla."
60. Mio Çid Roy Diaz odredes lo que dixo:
"comed, co*m*de, deste pan e beved deste vino.
"Si lo que digo fiziéredes, saldredes de cativo;
"si non, en todos vuestros días non veredes cristianismo."
61. "—Comede, don Rodrigo, e penssedes de folgar,
"que yo dexar mê morir, que non quiero comer *al.*"
Fasta terçer día nol pueden acordar;
ellos partiendo estas ganançias grandes,
nol pueden fazer comer un muesso de pan.
62. Dixo mio Çid: "comed, co*m*de, algo,
"ca si non comedes, non veredes cristianos;
"e si vos comiéredes don yo sea pagado,
"a vos, *el comde,* e dos fijos dalgo
"quitarvos e los cuerpos e darvos e de mano."
Quando esto oyó el co*m*de, yas iva alegrando:
"Si lo fiziéredes, Çid, lo que avedes fablado,
"tanto quanto yo biva, seré dent maravillado."
"—Pues comed, co*m*de, e quando fóredes yantado,
"a vos e a otros dos dar vos he de mano.
"Mas quanto avedes perdido e yo gané en canpo,
"sabet, non daré a vos *de ello* un dinero malo;
"ca huebos me lo he pora estos que comigo andan lazrados.
"Prendiendo de vos e de otros ir nos hemos pagando;
"abremos esta vida mientra ploguiere al Padre santo,
"commo que ira a de rey e de tierra es echado."
Alegre es el conde e pidió agua a las manos,
e tiénengelo delant e diérongelo privado.
Con los cavalleros que el Çid le avié dados
comiendo va el co*m*de ¡Dios, qué de buen grado!
Sobrél sedié el que en buen ora nasco:
"Si bien non comedes, co*m*de, don yo sea pagado,
"aquí feremos la morada, no nos partiremos amos."

and his men assembled around him on all sides;
My Cid was pleased because the spoils were great.
A banquet was prepared for My Cid Don Rodrigo;
Count Ramón showed no appreciation of it;
they brought him dishes, setting them down in front of him,
but he refused to eat, disdaining every one:
"I won't eat a morsel for all the wealth in Spain;
I'll sooner destroy my body and surrender my soul,
seeing that I've been bested in battle by men with such ugly footwear."
60. You shall hear what My Cid Ruy Díaz said:
"Eat of this bread, count, and drink of this wine.
If you do what I ask, you will get out of captivity;
if not, you won't see Christians again as long as you live."
61. "*You* eat, Don Rodrigo, and enjoy yourself,
but I will let myself die, I refuse to eat a thing."
Until the third day they couldn't get him to consent;
while they were sharing out those immense spoils,
they couldn't make him eat a mouthful of bread.
62. My Cid said: "Count, eat something,
for if you don't eat, you won't see Christian territory again;
but if you do eat to my satisfaction,
you, count, and two of your noblemen
I shall set free, and let you go."
When the count heard that, he began to take heart:
"If you do what you said, Cid,
I'll be amazed at it as long as I live."
"Well, then, eat, count, and after you've dined,
I shall release you and two others.
But of all that you lost and I won in the field,
I'll have you know I won't return a red cent,
because I need it for the men who joined my ranks as paupers.
By taking from you and others we will gradually mend our fortunes;
we will keep up this life as long as it pleases God the Father,
as befits men out of favor with their king and in exile."
The count, now cheerful, asked for water to wash his hands,
which they brought and presented to him swiftly.
Together with the knights whom the Cid had released to him
the count ate, and with what great pleasure!
He that was born in a lucky hour sat beside him:
"If you don't eat a lot, count, so that I am satisfied,
we will remain together right here, and won't part."

Aquí dixo el comde: "de voluntad e de grado."
Con estos dos cavalleros apriessa va yantando;
pagado es mio Çid, que lo está aguardando,
por que el comde don Remont tan bien bolvié las manos.
"Si vos ploguiere, mio Çid, de ir somos guisados;
"mandadnos dar las bestias e cavalgaremos privado;
"del día que fue comde non yanté tan de buen grado,
"el sabor que dend e non será olbidado."
Danles tres palafrés muy bien ensellados
e buenas vestiduras de pelliçones e de mantos.
El comde don Remont entre los dos es entrado.
Fata cabo del albergada escurriólos el Castellano:
"Ya vos ides, comde, a guisa de muy franco,
"en grado vos lo tengo lo que me avedes dexado.
"Si vos viniere emiente que quisiéredes vengallo,
"si me viniéredes buscar, fazedme antes mandado;
"o me dexaredes de lo vuestro, o de lo mio levaredes algo."
"—Folguedes, ya mio Çid, sodes en vuestro salvo.
"Pagado vos he por todo aqueste año;
"de venirvos buscar sol non será penssado."
63. Aguijaba el comde e penssava de andar,
tornando va la cabeça e catándos atrás;
miedo iva aviendo que mio Çid se repintrá,
lo que non ferié el caboso por quanto en el mundo ha,
una deslealtança ca non la fizo alguandre.
Ido es el comde, tornós el de Bivar,
juntós con sus mesnadas, conpeçós de alegrar
de la ganançia que han fecha maravillosa e grand;
tan ricos son los sos que non saben qué se an.

To which the count replied: "Readily and gladly!"
In the company of those two knights he wolfed down the food;
My Cid, who was observing him, was satisfied
at seeing Count Ramón make such good use of his hands.
"If it pleases you, My Cid, we are ready to leave;
have our mounts given to us and we shall ride at once;
since the day I became count I've never dined so gladly,
and I won't forget the taste of your meal."
They were given three palfreys with very good saddles
and fine outfits of pelisses and mantles.
Count Ramón took his place between the other two.
Up to the end of the camp they were escorted by the Castilian:
"Now, count, you are departing a totally free man;[16]
I thank you for all you have left behind with me.
If it ever occurs to you to take revenge for it
and you come after me, let me know in advance;
you'll leave some of your goods with me, or you'll take away some of mine."
"Be at ease, O My Cid, you're perfectly safe.
I've already given you a full year's payment;
I wouldn't even dream of coming after you."
63. The count spurred his horse and was about to go
when he turned his head and looked back,
fearing lest My Cid might change his mind,
which that excellent man wouldn't have done for anything in the world,
for he never committed a treacherous act.
The count departed; the lord of Vivar rode back
to join his troops and began to take delight
in the great, marvelous booty they had won;
his men were so wealthy they didn't know how much they had.

[SUMMARY of strophes **64–70** (verses 1085–1166):[17] Now the Cid
turns south and toward the sea, capturing fortresses in the northern
part of the Moorish realm of Valencia. The emir of Valencia sends an
army to besiege him in Sagunto, where the Cid wins another pitched
battle, thanks to strategy suggested by Álvar Fáñez. After that, the Cid
is able to take fortresses even south of the city of Valencia.]

---

16. A pun: *franco* also means "a Catalan." 17. Many editors begin a new subdivi-
sion (*"cantar segundo"*) of the *Poema* with strophe 64; on the possible subdivisions, see
the discussion in the Introduction.

[Tiradas 71–82 (versos 1167–1384):]

71. En tierra de moros prendiendo e ganando,
e durmiendo los días e las noches tranochando,
en ganar aquellas villas mio Çid duró tres años.
72. A los de Valençia escarmentados los han,
non osan fueras exir nin con él se ajuntar;
tajávales las huertas e fazíales grand mal,
en cada uno destos años mio Çid les tollió el pan.
Mal se aquexan los de Valençia que non sabent qués far,
de ninguna part que sea non les vinié pan;
nin de conssejo padre a fijo, nin fijo a padre,
nin amigo a amigo nos pueden consolar.
Mala cueta es, señores, aver mingua de pan,
fijos e mugieres veer los murir de fanbre.
Delante veyen so duelo, non se pueden huviar,
por el rey de Marruecos ovieron a enbiar;
con el de los Montes Claros avié guerra tan grand,
non les dixo consejo, nin los vino huviar.
Sópolo mio Çid, de coraçón le plaz;
salió de Murviedro una noch a trasnochar,
amaneció a mio Çid en tierras de Mon Real.
Por Aragón e por Navarra pregón mandó echar,
a tierras de Castiella enbió sos menssajes:
"Quien quiere perder cueta e venir a rritad,
"viniesse a mio Çid que a sabor de cavalgar;
"çercar quiere a Valençia pora cristianos la dar;
73. "quien quiere ir comigo çercar a Valençia,
"—todos vengan de grado, ninguno non ha premia,—
"tres días le speraré en Canal de Çelfa."
74. Esto dixo mio Çid el *Campeador leal.*
Tornávas a Murviedro, ca él ganada se la a.
Andidieron los pregones, sabet, a todas partes,
al sabor de la ganançia, non lo quieren detardar,
grandes yentes se le acojen de la buena cristiandad.
Sonando van sus nuevas todas a todas partes;
mas le vienen a mio Çid, sabet, que nos le van;
creçiendo va riqueza a mio Çid el de Bivar;
quando vido las gentes juntadas, compeçós de pagar.
Mio Çid don Rodrigo non lo quiso detardar,
adeliñó pora Valençia e sobrellas va echar,
bien la çerca mio Çid, que non i avía hart;

[**Strophes 71–82** (verses 1167–1384):]

71. Making seizures and gains in Moorish lands,
sleeping by day and marching by night,
My Cid spent three years conquering those towns.
72. He had put the fear of God in the inhabitants of Valencia,
who didn't dare to sally out and clash with him,
he ravaged their cultivated land, causing them great damage;
My Cid robbed them of their grain each of those years.
The people of Valencia, not knowing what to do, lamented;
grain for bread didn't come to them from anywhere;
father couldn't help son, or son father;
nor could one friend console another.
Gentlemen, it's a dire strait to be short of bread,
to see your children and wife dying of hunger.
Their grief was before their eyes, they couldn't help themselves,
so they decided to send for aid to the king of Morocco;
engaged in a major war with the king of the Atlas Mountains,
he was unable to offer assistance or come to their aid.
Learning this, My Cid was glad at heart;
one night he left Sagunto, marched all night,
and in the morning My Cid was in the vicinity of Monreal del Campo.
He had a proclamation made throughout Aragon and Navarre,
and sent his messengers to Castilian lands:
"Whoever wants to cast away poverty and become rich,
come to My Cid, who is eager to ride out;
he wants to besiege Valencia and give it to the Christians;
73. if anyone wishes to come with me to besiege Valencia—
let all come at their own pleasure, there's no compulsion—
I will be waiting for three days at Cella."
74. Thus spoke My Cid, the loyal Champion.
He returned to Sagunto, which he had conquered.
I'll have you know that his heralds traveled all over;
with a taste for gain, no one wanted to delay,
and many people came to join him from the good Christian lands.
All his exploits became known everywhere;
I'll have you know that more men joined My Cid than left his service;
the wealth of My Cid, lord of Vivar, kept increasing;
when he saw all those men assembled, he became happy.
My Cid Don Rodrigo brooked no delay,
he started out for Valencia and encircled it
with such a thorough siege that there was no escape;

viédales exir e viédales entrar.
Metióla en plaz*d*o, si les viniessen huviar.
Nueve meses complidos, sabet, sobrella yaz,
quando vino el dezeno oviérongela a dar.
Grandes son los gozos que van por es logar,
quando mio Çid gañó a Valençia e entró en la çibdad.
Los que foron de pie cavalleros se fazen;
el oro e la plata ¿quién vos lo podrié contar?
Todos eran ricos quantos que allí ha.
Mio Çid don Rodrigo la quinta mandó tomar,
en el aver monedado treynta mill marcos le caen,
e los otros averes ¿quién los podrié contar?
Alegre era el Campeador con todos los que ha,
quando su seña cabdal sedié en somo del alcáçer.
75. Ya folgava mio Çid con todas sus conpañas:
âquel rey de Sevilla el mandado llegava,
que presa es Valençia, que non gela enparan,
vino los veer atacar con treynta mill de armas.
Aprés de la uerta ovieron la batalla,
arrancólos mio Çid el de la luenga barba.
Fata dentro en Xátiva duró el arrancada,
en el passar de Xúcar i veriédes barata,
moros en arruenço amidos bever agua.
Aquel rey de *Sevilla* con tres colpes escapa.
Tornado es mio Çid con toda esta ganançia.
Buena fo la de Valençia quando ganaron la casa,
mas mucho fue provechosa, sabet, esta arrancada:
a todos los menores cayeron çient marcos de plata.
Las nuevas del cavallero ya veedes do llegavan.
76. Grand alegría es entre todos essos cristianos
con mio Çid Roy Díaz, el que en buen ora nasco.
Yal creçe la barba e vale allongando;
ca dixera mio Çid de la su boca atanto:
"por amor de rey Alffonsso, que de tierra me a echado"
nin entrarié en ella tigera, ni un pelo non avrié tajado,
e que fablassen desto moros e cristianos.
Mio Çid don Rodrigo en Valençia está folgando,
con él Minaya Álbar Fáñez que nos le parte de so braço.
Los que exieron de tierra de ritad son abondados,

he prevented them from going out or coming in.
He gave them a deadline for surrender if no one came to aid them sooner.
Nine full months, I'll have you know, he besieged that city;
when the tenth month began, they were obliged to yield it to him.
Great was the joy which spread through that place
when My Cid won Valencia and entered the city.
Those who had been foot soldiers became horsemen;
as for the gold and silver, who could count it?
Everyone there was rich.
My Cid Don Rodrigo collected his fifth;
in coined money, thirty thousand marks fell to his lot,
and as for the other possessions, who could count them?
The Champion and all the men with him were happy
when his personal banner waved at the summit of the citadel.
75. Now My Cid and all his companies rested:
the news reached the Moorish governor of Seville
that Valencia was taken and was not being protected for him;
he came to attack them with thirty thousand armed men.
The battle took place near the cultivated plain,
and was won by My Cid of the long beard.
The losers were pursued all the way to Játiva;
on crossing the Júcar river, a skirmish was to be seen,
with Moors against the current unwillingly drinking water.
That king of Seville[18] got off with three wounds.
My Cid returned with all that booty.
When the city of Valencia was taken, the spoils were great,
but I'll have you know that those from this victory were much greater:
each of the mere foot soldiers received a hundred marks of silver.
You can see how far the knight's fame extended.
76. There was great joy among all those Christians
and My Cid Ruy Díaz, the man born in a lucky hour.
His beard had been growing and getting longer;
for My Cid's lips had uttered the following words:
"For the love of King Alfonso, who exiled me,
no scissors shall touch it, and not one hair of it will be cut;
let Moors and Christians say what they like about this."
My Cid Don Rodrigo was relaxing in Valencia;
with him was Minaya Álvar Fáñez, who never strayed from his side.
Those who had left their homeland were abundantly rich;

18. Many editors now retain the MS reading *Marruecos*, explaining that the governor of Seville, who is meant, did come from Morocco.

a todos les dio en Valençia *el Campeador contado*
casas y heredades de que son pagados;
el amor de mio Çid ya lo ivan provando.
Los que foron después todos son pagados;
veelo mio Çid que con los averes que avién tomados,
que sis pudiessen ir, fer lo ien de grado.
Esto mandó mio Çid, Minaya lo ovo conssejado:
que ningún omne de los sos *que con él ganaron algo*
ques le non spidiés, o nol besás la mano,
sil pudiessen prender o fosse alcançado,
tomássenle el aver e pusiéssenle en un palo.
Afevos todo aquesto puesto en buen recabdo;
con Minaya Álbar Fáñez él se va conseja*ndo:*
"si vos quisiéredes, Minaya, quiero saber recabdo
"de los que son aquí e comigo ganaron algo;
"meterlos he en escripto, e todos sean contados,
"que si algunos furtare o menos le fallar*o*,
"el aver me avrá a tornar, âquestos myos vasallos
"que curian a Valençia e andan arrobdando."
Allí dixo Minaya: "consejo es aguisado."
77. Mandólos venir a la corth e a todos los juntar,
quando los falló por cuenta fízolos nonbrar;
tres mill e seys çientos avié mio Çid el de Bivar;
alégrasle el coraçón e tornós a sonrrisar:
"¡Grado a Dios, Minaya, e a santa María madre!
"con más pocos ixiemos de la casa de Bivar.
"Agora avemos riquiza, más avremos adelant.
"Si a vos ploguiere, Minaya, e non vos caya en pesar,
"enbiar vos quiero a Castiella, do avemos heredades,
"al rey Alfonsso mio señor natural;
"destas mis ganançias, que avemos fechas acá,
"dar le quiero çient cavallos, e vos ídgelos levar;
"desí por mí besalde la mano e firme gelo rogad
"por mi mugier *doña Ximena* e mis fijas *naturales,*
"si fore su merçed quenlas dexe sacar.
"Enbiaré por ellas, e vos sabed el mensage:
"la mugier de mio Çid e sus fijas las iffantes

in Valencia the Champion gave them all
houses and estates which satisfied them;
they were now experiencing My Cid's love.
Those who joined him later[19] were all satisfied, too.
My Cid realized that, with the possessions they had accumulated,
they would gladly depart if they could.
My Cid decreed, taking Minaya's advice,
that none of his men who had gained wealth under him
was to leave without a formal discharge and the ceremony of kissing his hand;
if anyone did and was overtaken and captured,
his wealth was to be confiscated and he was to be hanged.
See, all of this was now put in good order;
taking further counsel with Minaya Álvar Fáñez:
"If you don't mind, Minaya, I'd like to take a census
of those who are here and have gained wealth under me;
I shall write their names down, and count them all,
and if anyone slips away and turns up missing,
his property will revert to me and to these vassals of mine
who are guarding Valencia and going out on patrol."
Minaya then said: "It's a wise plan."
77. He ordered everyone to assemble in a large hall;
when they were there, he had them counted;
My Cid, lord of Vivar, had thirty-six hundred men;
he was glad at heart and he smiled:
"I thank God, Minaya, and his mother the Blessed Virgin!
We left our homes in Vivar with many fewer.
Now we are wealthy, and will be more so in the future.
If it pleases you, Minaya, and you have no objection,
I want to send you to Castile, where we have estates,
to my feudal lord King Alfonso;
from the gains which we have made here
I wish to give him a hundred horses, and you are to take them to him;
then, in my behalf, kiss his hand and firmly request from him
my wife Doña Jimena and my dear daughters,
if he is gracious enough to release them to me.
I will send for them, and here is the message:
'The wife of My Cid and his young daughters

---

19. In the MS, *los que fueron con él e los de después* ("both those who left Castile at the same time as he did, and those who joined him later"). The text reprinted here makes the change in this line, and a few others, to establish a differentiation between the two groups.

"de guisa irán por ellas que a grand ondra vernán
"a esas tierras estrañas que nos pudiemos ganar."
Essora dixo Minaya: "de buena voluntad."
Pues esto an fablado, piénssanse de adobar.
Ciento omnes le dio mio Çid a Álbar Fáñez
por servirle en la carrera *a toda su voluntad,*
e mandó mill marcos de plata a San Pero levar
e que los *quinientos* diesse a don Sancho el abbat.
78. En estas nuevas todos se alegrando,
de parte de orient vino un coronado;
el obispo don Jero*me* so nombre es llamado.
Bien entendido es de letras e mucho acordado,
de pie e de cavallo mucho era arreziado.
Las provezas de mio Çid andávalas demandando,
sospirando ques viesse con moros en el campo:
que sis fartás lidiando e firiendo con sus manos,
a los días del sieglo non le llorassen cristianos.
Quando lo oyó mio Çid, de aquesto *fo* pagado:
"Oíd, Minaya Álbar Fáñez, por aquel que está en alto,
"quando Dios prestar nos quiere, nos bien gelo gradescamos:
"es tierras de Valençia fer quiero obispado,
"e dárgelo a este buen cristiano;
"vos, quando ides a Castiella, levaredes buenos mandados."
79. Plogo a Álbar Fáñez de lo que dixo don Rodrigo.
A este don Jero*me* yal otorgan por obispo;
diéronle en Valençia o bien puede estar rico.
¡Dios, qué alegre era tod cristianismo,
que en tierras de Valençia señor avié obispo!
Alegre *fo* Minaya e spidiós e vinos.
80. Tierras de Valençia remanidas en paz,
adeliñó pora Castiella Minaya Álbar Fáñez.
Dexarévos las posadas, non las quiero contar.
Demandó por Alfonsso, do lo podrié fallar.
F*o*ra el rey a San Fagunt aun poco ha,
tornós a Carrión, i lo podrié fallar.
Alegre *fo* de aquesto Minaya Álbar Fáñez,
con esta present*a*ja adeliñó pora allá.
81. De missa era exido essora el rey Alfonsso.
Afe Minaya Álbar Fáñez do llega tan apu*o*sto:

will be sent for in such a fashion that they will come in great honor
to those foreign lands which we have been able to conquer.'"
Then Minaya said: "Gladly."
Having discussed this, they began to make preparations.
My Cid gave Álvar Fáñez a hundred men
to cater to his every wish on the journey,
and ordered a thousand marks of silver brought to San Pedro de Cardeña,
of which five hundred were for Don Sancho, the abbot.
78. While they were all happy at those events,
a priest arrived from Eastern parts;
his name was Bishop Jérôme.
He was a learned and a very wise man,
very hardy on foot and on horseback.
He kept asking about My Cid's exploits,
yearning to give battle to Moors in the field,
and saying that, if he could have his fill of physical fighting and action,
no one need ever mourn his death as long as the world lasted.
When My Cid heard this, he was pleased:
"Listen, Minaya Álvar Fáñez, by the Lord in heaven,
when God is willing to assist us, we should be very grateful:
I want to create a bishopric in Valencian territory,
and give it to this good Christian;
when you go to Castile, take along those good messages."
79. Álvar Fáñez was pleased at what Don Rodrigo said.
This Don Jérôme was now accepted as bishop;
he was installed in Valencia, where he could readily grow rich.
Lord, how happy every Christian was
to hear that there was a bishop in Valencian territory!
Minaya was glad; he took his leave and departed.
80. With the Valencian lands pacified,
Minaya Álvar Fáñez set out for Castile.
I will spare you his stopping places, I don't want to enumerate them.
He asked the whereabouts of Alfonso, where he could find him.
The king had gone to Sahagún shortly before,
then had come back as far as Carrión de los Condes; he could find him there.
Minaya Álvar Fáñez was glad to hear this,
and set out for that town with his gift.
81. King Alfonso had just finished hearing mass
when there was Minaya Álvar Fáñez, arriving so opportunely![20]

---

20. Or: "so well dressed."

fincó sos inojos ante tod el puoblo,
a los piedes del rey Alfons cayó con grand duolo,
besávale las manos e fabló tan apuosto:
82. "¡Merced, señor Alfonsso, por amor del Criador!
"¡Besávavos las manos mio Çid lidiador,
"los piedes e las manos, commo a tan buen señor,
"quel ayades merçed sí vos vala el Criador!
"Echástesle de tierra, non ha la vuestra amor:
"maguer en tierra agena, él bien faze lo so:
"ganada a Xérica e a Onda por nombre,
"priso a Almenar e a Murviedro que es miyor,
"assí fizo Çebolla e adelant Castejón,
"e Peña Cadiella, que es una peña fuort;
"con aquestas todas de Valençia es señor,
"obispo fizo de su mano el buen Campeador,
"e fizo çinco lides campales e todas las arrancó.
"Grandes son las ganançias quel dio el Criador,
"fevor aquí las señas, verdad vos digo yo:
"çient cavallos gruessos e corredores,
"de siellas e de frenos todos guarnidos son,
"bésavos las manos que los prendades vos;
"razonas por vuestro vasallo e a vos tiene por señor."
Alçó la mano diestra, el rey se santigó:
"De tan fieras ganançias commo a fechas el Campeador
"¡sí me vala sant Esidre! plázme de coraçón,
"e plázme de las nuevas que faze el Campeador;
"reçibo estos cavallos quem enbía de don."
Maguer plogo al rey, mucho pesó a Garci Ordóñez:
"¡Semeja que en tierra de moros non a bivo omne,
"quando assí faze a su guisa el Çid Campeador!"
Dixo el rey al comde: "dexad essa razón,
"que en todas guisas mijor me sirva que vos."
Fablava Minaya i a guisa de varón:
"merçed vos pide el Çid, si vos cadiesse en sabor,
"por su mugier doña Ximena e sus fijas amas a dos
"saldrién del monesterio do elle las dexó,
"e irién pora Valençia, al buen Campeador."
Essora dixo el rey: "Plazme de coraçone;
"yo les mandaré dar conducho mientra que por mi tierra foren,
"de fonta e de mal curiallas e de desonore;
"quando en cabo de mi tierra aquestas dueñas foren,

He knelt down before all the populace,
falling at King Alfonso's feet in great travail;
he kissed his hands and spoke elegantly:
82. "Be gracious, King Alfonso, for the love of the Creator!
My Cid the battler kisses your hands,
your feet and hands, since you are such a good lord,
begging for grace (so may the Creator keep you!).
You exiled him, he is deprived of your love:
though on foreign soil, he is still acting nobly:
he has taken the towns called Jérica and Onda,
he has captured Almenara and Sagunto, which is better,
as well as Puig and then Castellón de la Plana,
and Benicadell, which is a fortified crag;
in addition to all those, he is master of Valencia,
and the good Champion has appointed a bishop,
and has fought five pitched battles and won them all.
Great are the spoils which the Creator has given him;
here is proof of it, I tell you the truth:
a hundred stout, swift horses,
all furnished with saddles and bits;
he kisses your hands and begs you to accept them;
he counts himself your vassal and deems you his lord."
Raising his right hand, the king crossed himself:
"For these amazing profits which the Champion has made
(so may Saint Isidore of Seville keep me!) I am heartily glad!
And I am happy for the exploits the Champion is performing;
I accept these horses he sends me as a gift."
Though the king was pleased, Garci Ordóñez was greatly vexed:
"Apparently there isn't a living man in Moorish territory
if the Cid and Champion can do just as he likes in this way!"
The king said to the count: "Cease speaking like that,
because, whatever his way is, he's doing me greater service than you are."
Then Minaya spoke manfully:
"The Cid beseeches you, if you should so please,
to let his wife Doña Jimena and both his daughters
leave the monastery where he left them
and go to Valencia to rejoin the good Champion."
Then the king said: "I am heartily pleased;
I shall have them provisioned as long as they are in my territory,
and shall see them protected from insult, harm, and dishonor;
when those ladies reach the boundary of my realm,

"catad cómmo las sirvades vos e el Campeador*e*.
"¡Oídme, escuelas, e toda la mi cort!
"non quiero que nada pierda el Campeador;
"a todas las escuelas que a él dizen señor
"por que los deseredé, todo gelo suelto yo;
"sírvanle' sus her*e*dades do f*o*re el Campeador,
"atrégoles los cuerpos de mal e de ocasión,
"por tal fago aquesto que sirvan a so señor."
Minaya Álbar Fáñez las manos le besó.
Sonrrisós el rey, tan vellido fabló:
"Los que quisieren ir se*r*vir al Campeador
"de mí sean quitos e vayan a la gra*ç*ia del Criador.
"Más ganaremos en esto que en otra des*amor*."
Aquí entraron en fabla iffantes de Carrión:
"Mucho cre*ç*en las nuevas de mio *Ç*id el Campeador,
"bien casariemos con sus fijas pora huebos de pro.
"Non la osariemos acometer nos esta razón;
"mio *Ç*id es de Bivar e nos de co*m*des de Carrión."
Non lo dizen a nadi, e fincó esta razón.
Minaya Álbar Fáñez al buen rey se espidió.
"¿Hya vos ides, Minaya? ¡id a la gra*ç*ia del Criador!
"Levedes un portero, tengo que vos avrá pro;
"si leváredes las dueñas, sírvanlas a su sabor,
"fata dentro en Medina denles quanto huebos les f*o*r,
"desí adelant piensse dellas el Campeador."
Espidiós Minaya e vasse de la cort.

it will be up to you and the Champion to look after them.
Listen, my retinue, and all my court!
I don't want the Champion to lose a thing;
to all the troops that call him their lord
I restore all the property of which I had deprived them;
wherever they may be in the Champion's service, let them have the use of their estates;
I guarantee their persons against harm and injury;
I do so in order that they may serve their master."
Minaya Álvar Fáñez kissed his hands.
The king smiled and spoke beautifully:
"Any and all who wish to go and serve the Champion
shall be exempt from serving me and may depart in the Creator's grace.
We shall gain more by this than by hostility."
Then the young lords of Carrión began to confer:
"The affairs of My Cid the Champion are improving greatly;
we would do well to marry his daughters for our advantage.
We wouldn't dare to utter this suggestion:
My Cid is merely from Vivar, while we are counts of Carrión."
They told no one else about it, and that conversation ended.
Minaya Álvar Fáñez took leave of the good king.
"Are you already leaving, Minaya? Go in the Creator's grace!
Take along a royal commissioner, I think you'll find him useful;
if you take the ladies with you, let them be looked after at their pleasure;
let them be given all they need until they reach Medinaceli;
from then on, let the Champion take care of them."
Minaya said good-bye and left the court.

[SUMMARY of strophes **83 & 84** (verses 1385–1561): As Álvar Fáñez departs, the young lords of Carrión give him a message for the Cid: they will act to his advantage, and they desire his favor. From San Pedro de Cardeña, Álvar Fáñez sends word to the Cid that his family is on the way. More men join him. In Burgos the moneylenders ask him to return the loan, even without interest; he promises to discuss it with the Cid. (Nothing more is ever said about it.) Learning that his family has reached the Castilian border, the Cid, who must stay in Valencia to protect it, sends men to ask the aid of the friendly Moorish ruler of Molina de Aragón, Ibn Ghalbun; the Moor escorts the Cid's family to Valencia, along with Álvar Fáñez and other men, including the bishop, sent out by the Cid.]

[**Tiradas 85–90** (versos 1562–1656):]
85. Alegre *fo* mio Çid, que nunqua más nin tanto,
ca de lo que más amava yál viene el mandado.
Dozie*n*tos cavalleros mandó exir privado,
que reciban a Minaya e a las dueñas fijas dalgo:
él sedié en Valençia curiando e guardando,
ca bien sabe que Álbar Fáñez trahe todo recabdo;
86. afevos todos aquestos reçiben a Minaya
e a las dueñas e a las niñas e a las otras conpañas.
Mandó mio Çid a los que ha en su*e* casa
que guardassen el alcáçer en las otras torres altas
e todas las puertas e las exidas e las entradas,
e aduxiéssenle a Bavieca; poco avié quel ganara
d' aquel rey de Sevilla e de la sue arrancada,
aun non sabié mio Çid, el que en buen ora çinxo espada,
si serié corredor o ssi abrié buena parada;
a la puerta de Valençia, do en so salvo *estava,*
delante su mugier e de sus fijas querié tener las armas.
Reçebidas las dueñas a una grant ondrança,
obispo don Jero*me* adelant se entrava,
y dexava el cavallo, pora la capiella adeliñava;
con quantos que él puede, que con oras se acordar*a*n,
sobrepelliças vestidas e con cruzes de plata,
reçibir salién las dueñas e al bueno de Minaya.
El que en buen ora nasco non lo detardava:
vistiós el sobregonel; luenga trahe la barba;
ensiéllanle a Bavieca, cuberturas le echavan,
mio Çid salió sobrél, e armas de fuste tomava.
Por nombre el cavallo Bavieca cavalga,
fizo una corrida, ésta *fo* tan estraña,
quando ovo corrido, todos se maravillavan;
des día se preçió Bavieca en quant grant *fo* España.
En cabo del cosso mio Çid desca*v*algava,
adeliñó a su mugier e a su*es* fijas amas;
quando lo vio doña Ximena, a pie*des* se le echava:
"¡Merced, Campeador, en buen ora cinxiestes espada!
"Sacada me avedes de muchas vergüenças malas;

[**Strophes 85–90** (verses 1562–1656):]

85. My Cid was happier than ever,
for he had now received word about those he loved most.
He ordered two hundred horsemen to ride out swiftly
to welcome Minaya and the noble ladies:
he remained in Valencia to watch and guard it,
well aware that Álvar Fáñez was taking every precaution.
86. Behold, all those horsemen welcomed Minaya
and the ladies and the girls and the other troops.
My Cid ordered those in his household
to guard the citadel on the other high towers
and all gates, exits, and entrances,
and to bring him Babieca;[21] he had won him recently
when he defeated that governor of Seville;
My Cid, he that girded on his sword in a lucky hour, did not yet know
whether the horse was a fast runner or could stop short when necessary;
at the Valencia city gate, where he was in safety,
he wished to display his skill in arms to his wife and daughters.
After the ladies were welcomed with great honors,
Bishop Jérôme rode in,
dismounted, and headed for the chapel;
with as many priests as he could find (having rearranged the canonical hours),[22]
all wearing surplices and carrying silver crosses,
he went out to greet the ladies and good Minaya.
He that was born in a lucky hour made no delay:
he put on his surcoat (his beard was long);
Babieca was saddled for him and covered with trappings;
My Cid mounted him and grasped wooden weapons.
He rode the horse called Babieca
at a speed so extraordinary
that everyone marveled after his run;
from then on Babieca was esteemed from one end of Spain to another.
At the end of the sprint My Cid dismounted,
approaching his wife and his two daughters;
when Doña Jimena saw him, she threw herself at his feet:
"Thank you, Champion, you that girded on your sword in a lucky hour!
You have rescued me from many grave affronts;

---

21. The horse's name means "simpleton" nowadays, but most likely connoted "froth-
ing at the mouth."   22. Or: "having been notified in advance"; or: "in accordance with
the time of day."

"afeme aquí, señor, yo e vuestras fijas amas,
"con Dios e convusco buenas son e criadas."
A la madre e a las fijas bien las abraçava,
del gozo que avién de los sos ojos lloravan.
Todas las sus mesnadas en grant deleyt estavan,
armas tenién e tablados crebantavan.
Oíd lo que dixo el que en buena çinxo espada:
"vos doña Ximena, querida mugier e ondrada,
"e amas mis fijas mio coraçón e mi alma,
"entrad comigo en Valençia la casa,
"en esta heredad que vos yo he ganada."
Madre e fijas las manos le besavan.
A tan grand ondra ellas a Valençia entravan.
87. Adeliñó mio Çid con ellas al alcáçer,
allá las subié en el más alto logar.
Ojos vellidos catan a todas partes,
miran Valençia cómmo yaze la çibdad,
e del otra parte a ojo han el mar,
miran la huerta, espessa es e grand,
e todas las otras cosas que eran de solaz;
alçan las manos pora Dios rogar,
desta ganançia cómmo es buena e grand.
Mio Çid e sus compañas tan a grand sabor están.
El ivierno es exido, que el março quiere entrar.
Dezir vos quiero nuevas de allent partes del mar,
de aquel rey Yúcef que en Marruecos está.
88. Pesól al rey de Marruecos de mio Çid don Rodrigo:
"que en mis heredades fuertemientre es metido,
"e él non gelo gradeçe sinon a Jesu Cristo."
Aquel rey de Marruecos ajuntava sus virtos;
con çinquaenta vezes mill de armas, todos foron conplidos,
entraron sobre mar, en las barcas son metidos,
van buscar a Valençia a mio Çid don Rodrigo.
Arribado an las naves, fuera eran exidos.
89. Llegaron a Valençia, la que mio Çid a conquista,
fincaron las tiendas, e posan las yentes descreidas.
Estas nuevas a mio Çid eran venidas.
90. "¡Grado al Criador e al Padre espirital!

here I am, my lord, I and your two daughters,
who are good and well brought up, thanks to you and God."
He hugged mother and daughters tightly,
and they all wept with joy.
All his troops were highly delighted;
they took up arms and toppled *tablados*.[23]
Hear what he that girded on his sword in a lucky hour said:
"You, Doña Jimena, my beloved and honored wife,
and my two daughters, my heart and soul,
enter with me into the city of Valencia,
this property which I have won for you."
Mother and daughters kissed his hands.
With great honors they entered Valencia.

87. My Cid went to the citadel with them;
there he led them up to the loftiest spot.
Their lovely eyes gazed in every direction;
they looked at the layout of Valencia;
on the other side, they could view the sea;
they looked at the cultivated land, which was large and luxuriant,
and at all the other pleasurable things.
They raised their hands to thank God
for that fine, great conquest.
My Cid and his troops were filled with pleasure.
Winter had gone, and March was about to begin.
Now I wish to inform you of doings overseas,
about that king Yusuf in Morocco.

88. The king of Morocco was grieved at My Cid Don Rodrigo:
"For he has brazenly intruded onto my lands,
and the only one he thanks for it is Jesus Christ!"
That king of Morocco assembled his forces;
with fifty thousand armed men their number was complete;[24]
they embarked and set sail,
bound for Valencia to attack My Cid Don Rodrigo.
the ships landed and they disembarked.

89. They reached Valencia, which My Cid had conquered;
the infidels pitched their tents and encamped.
News of this reached My Cid.

90. "I thank the Creator, my Father in heaven!

---

23. The equivalent of quintains elsewhere, Spanish *tablados* were wooden scaffolds on poles to be tilted at, or assailed with hurled darts, for training and for sport.
24. Or: "50,000 armed men, all of them excellent."

"Todo el bien que yo he, todo lo tengo delant:
"con afán gané a Valençia, e ela por heredad,
"a menos de muert no la puodo dexar;
"grado al Criador e a santa María madre
"mis fijas e mi mugier que las tengo acá.
"Venídom es deliçio de tierras d' allent mar,
"entraré en las armas, non lo podré dexar;
"mis fijas e mi mugier veerme an lidiar;
"en estas tierras agenas verán las moradas cómmo se fazen,
"afarto verán por los ojos cómmo se gana el pan."
Su mugier e sus fijas subiólas al alcáçer,
alçavan los ojos, tiendas, vidieron fincar:
"¿Quês esto, Çid? ¡sí el Criador vos salve!"
"—¡Ya mugier ondrada, non ayades pesar!
"Riqueza es que nos acreçe maravillosa e grand:
"a poco que viniestes, presend vos quieren dar:
"por casar son vuestras fijas, adúzenvos axuvar."
"—A vos grado, Çid, e al Padre spirital."
"—Mugier, seed en este palaçio, en el alcáçer;
"non ayades pavor por que me veades lidiar,
"con la merced de Dios e de santa María madre,
"créçem el coraçón por que estades delant;
"con Dios aquesta lid yo la he de arrancar."

[**Tiradas 96–103** (versos 1799–1984):]
96. Alegres son por Valençia las yentes cristianas,
tantos avién de averes, de cavallos e de armas;
alegre es doña Ximena e sus fijas amas,
e todas las otras dueñas ques tienen por casadas.
El bueno de mio Çid non lo tardó por nada:

All that I possess I have before me:
I won Valencia through toil and hold it as my property;
I can't let it go while I live;
I thank the Creator and the Blessed Virgin
that I have my daughters and wife here.
A gift has come to me from overseas;
I shall combat them, I can't avoid it;
my daughters and wife will watch me fight;
they'll see what life is like in these foreign lands,
and they'll see all too well for themselves how I earn my bread."
He had his wife and daughters ascend the citadel;
raising their eyes, they saw tents being pitched:
"What is all this, Cid? May the Creator save you!"
"O my honored wife, do not be upset!
It is wealth, wondrous and grand, which we are gaining:
you have just come and they want to give you a present:
your daughters are ready to marry, and they're bringing you a dowry."
"I thank you, Cid, and our Father in heaven."
"Wife, remain in this palace, in the citadel;
have no fear if you see me fighting;
with the grace of God and his mother the Blessed Virgin,
my heart swells at seeing you before me:
with God's help I shall win this battle."

[SUMMARY of strophes **91–95** (verses 1657–1798): On the first day of battle the Cid beats back the Moorish attack. For the next day, Álvar Fáñez suggests a surprise attack, after the start of battle, by a reserve detachment. Before dawn, the bishop sings mass and gives absolution; he then asks the Cid to let him lead the charge. The Cid's army of under 4,000 defeat the huge Moorish army in the battle of Cuarto. King Yusuf escapes; the Cid sends his rich tent to King Alfonso, and gives the bishop a tenth (tithe) of his own fifth part of the spoils. He enriches Jimena's loyal ladies-in-waiting and promises to marry them to vassals of his.]

[Strophes 96–103 (verses 1799–1984):]

96. The Christian folk in Valencia were happy,
they had so many possessions, horses, and weapons;
Doña Jimena and her two daughters were happy,
and all the other ladies, who were as good as married.
My good Cid made no delay:

"¿Do sodes, caboso? venid acá, Minaya;
"de lo que a vos cadió vos non gradeçedes nada;
"desta mi quinta, dígovos sin falla,
"prended lo que quisiéredes, lo otro remanga.
"E cras ha la mañana ir vos hedes sin falla
"con cavallos desta quinta que yo he ganada,
"con siellas e con frenos e con señas espadas;
"por amor de mi mugier e de mis fijas amas,
"por que assí las enbió dond ellas son pagadas,
"estos dozientos cavallos irán en presentajas,
"que non diga mal el rey Alfons del que Valençia manda."
Mandó a Per Vermudoz que fosse con Minaya.
Otro día mañana privado cavalgavan,
e dozientos omnes lievan en su conpaña,
con saludes del Çid que las manos le besava:
desta lid que *mio Çid* ha arrancada
dozientos cavallos le enbiava en presentaja,
"e servir lo he sienpre mientra que ovisse el alma."
97. Salidos son de Valençia e pienssan de andar,
tales ganancias traen que son a aguardar.
Andan los días e las noches, *que vagar non se dan,*
e passada han la sierra, que las otras tierras parte.
Por el rey don Alfons tómanse a preguntar.
98. Passando van las sierras e los montes e las aguas,
llegan a Valladolid do el rey Alfons estava;
enviávale mandado Per Vermudoz e Minaya,
que mandasse reçebir a esta conpaña,
mio Çid el de Valençia enbía sue presentaja.
99. Alegre fo el rey, non vidiestes atanto,
mandó cavalgar apriessa todos sos fijos dalgo
i en los primeros el rey fuera dió salto,
a veer estos mensajes del que en buen ora nasco.
Ifantes de Carrión, sabet, is açertaron,
e comde don García, *del Çid* so enemigo malo.
A los unos plaze e a los otros va pesando.
A ojo los avién los del que en buen ora nasco,
cuédanse que es almofalla, ca non vienen con mandado;
el rey don Alfonso seíse santiguando.
Minaya e Per Vermudoz adelante son llegados,
firiéronse a tierra, diçieron de los cavallos;
antel rey Alfons los inoios fincados,

"Where are you, excellent man? Come here, Minaya;
for your share of the spoils you are beholden to no one;
I tell you truly, from my fifth part
take whatever you want and leave the rest.
And tomorrow morning without fail you must depart
with horses from this fifth I have won,
each with a saddle, bit, and sword;
in the name of my wife and my two daughters,
because he has sent them here where they are contented,
these two hundred horses will go as a gift,
so King Alfonso won't speak badly of the ruler of Valencia."
He ordered Pedro Bermúdez to go with Minaya.
The next morning they rode off swiftly,
with an escort of two hundred men,
bearing greetings from the Cid, who kissed the king's hands:
from that battle which the Cid won
he was sending him two hundred horses as a gift,
"and I shall always serve him as long as I live."
97. They set out from Valencia and began their journey,
bringing such great treasure it had to be guarded.
They traveled days and nights, allowing themselves no respite,
and they crossed the mountain range that bounded those other lands.
They started to inquire after King Alfonso's whereabouts.
98. They continued to cross mountains, forests, and rivers
until they reached Valladolid, where the king then was;
Pedro Bermúdez and Minaya sent him word
to have their company met;
My Cid, lord of Valencia, was sending him a gift.
99. The king was pleased, never more so;
he ordered all his noblemen to ride out quickly,
and among the foremost the king galloped forth
to meet those messengers of the man born in a lucky hour.
I'll have you know that the young lords of Carrión were among them,
and Count García, the Cid's bitter enemy.
Some were pleased, while others were grieved.
They caught sight of the envoys of the man born in a lucky hour,
fearing it was a hostile army because they were arriving without notice;
King Alfonso kept crossing himself.
Minaya and Pedro Bermúdez rode out ahead
and touched ground, dismounting;
kneeling before King Alfonso,

besan la tierra e los pie*des* amos:
"¡Merced, rey Alfonsso, sodes tan ondrado!
"por mio Çid el Campeador todo esto vos besamos;
"a vos llama por señor, e tienes por vuestro vassallo,
"mucho preçia la ondra el Çid quel avedes dado.
"Pocos días ha, rey, que una lid a arrancado:
"a aquel rey de Marruecos, Yúceff por nombrado,
"con çinquaenta mill arrancólos del campo.
"L*os* ganad*os* que fizo mucho son sobejan*os*,
"ricos son venidos todos los sos vassallos,
"e embíavos dozientos cavallos, e bésavos las manos."
Dixo rey don Alfons: "Reçíbolos de grado.
"Gradéscolo a mio Çid que tal don me ha enbiado;
"aun vea ora que de mí sea pagado."
Esto plogo a muchos e besáronle las manos.
Pesó al co*m*de don García, e mal era irado;
con diez de s*os* parientes aparte davan salto:
"¡Maravilla es del Çid, que su ondra creçe tanto!
"En la ondra que él ha nos seremos abiltados;
"por tan biltadamientre vençer reyes del campo,
"commo si los fallase muertos aduzirse las cavallos,
"por esto que él faze nos abremos enbargo."
100. Fabló el rey don Alfons, *odredes lo que diz:*
"Grado al Criador e a señor sant Esidr*e*
"estos dozientos cavallos quem enbía mio Çid.
"Mio reyno adelant mejor me podrá servir.
"A vos Minaya Álbar Fáñez e a Per Vermu*doz* aquí
"mándovos los cuorpos ondradamientre vestir
"e guarnirvos de todas armas commo vos dixiéredes aquí,
"que bien parescades ante R*oy* Díaz mio Çid;
"dovos tres cavallos e prendedlos aquí.
"Assí commo semeja e la veluntad me lo diz,
"todas estas nuevas a bien abrán de venir."
101. Besáronle las manos y entraron a posar;
bien los mandó servir de quanto huebos han.
D' iffantes de Carrión yo vos quiero contar,
fablando en s*o* conssejo, aviendo su poridad:
"Las nuevas del Çid mucha van adelant,
"demandemos sus fijas pora con ellas casar;

they kissed the earth and his two feet:
"Grace, King Alfonso, you that are so honored!
In behalf of My Cid the Champion we ask you to accept all this;
he calls you his lord and deems himself your vassal;
the Cid esteems highly the honor you have shown him.
Quite recently, sire, he won a battle:
that king of Morocco named Yusuf
and his fifty thousand men he drove from the field.
The booty he seized is countless,
all of his vassals have become rich,
and he sends you two hundred horses, and kisses your hands."
King Alfonso said: "I accept them gladly.
I thank My Cid for sending me such a gift;
may I yet see a time when he has reason to be pleased with me."[25]
This speech contented many, who kissed his hands.
It vexed Count García, who was irate;
he quickly rode to one side with ten of his kinsmen:
"It's amazing how the Cid's honor is increasing so!
In his new honor *we* will be cheapened;
because such a lowborn man vanquishes kings in battle,
and rounds up their horses as if they were dead men,
for these doings of his we will suffer loss."
100. King Alfonso spoke (you shall hear what he said):
"I thank the Creator and Saint Isidore
for these two hundred horses My Cid has sent me.
He will be able to serve me even better as my reign progresses.
You, Minaya Álvar Fáñez, and Pedro Bermúdez here,
I order that your persons be clad in outfits of honor,
and that you be furnished with any armor you request,
so that you make a fine appearance before Ruy Díaz My Cid;
I give each of you three horses; take them here.
As it seems to me and my heart tells me,
all these events will turn out well."
101. They kissed his hands and sought their lodgings;
he ordered his men to serve them well with whatever they needed.
Now I want to tell you about the young lords of Carrión,
who were conferring together in privacy:
"The Cid's affairs are thriving greatly,
let us ask for his daughters' hand in marriage;

---

25. Or: "when I can repay him."

"creçremos en nuestra ondra e iremos adelant."
Vinién al rey Alfons con esta poridad:
102. Merced vos pidimos commo a rey e a señor;
"con vuestro conssejo lo queremos fer nos,
"que nos demandedes fijas del Campeador;
"casar queremos con ellas a su ondra y a nuestra pro."
Un grant ora el rey penssó e comidió;
"Yo eché de tierra al buen Campeador,
"e faziendo yo a él mal, e él a mí grand pro,
"del casamiento non sé sis abrá sabor;
"mas pues bos lo queredes, entremos en la razón."
A Minaya Álbar Fáñez e a Per Vermu*doz*
el rey don Alfonsso essora los llamó,
a una quadra elle los apartó:
"Oídme Minaya e vos, Per Vermu*doz:*
"sírvem mio Çid *Roi Díaz* Campeador,
"el*le* lo mereçe e de mí abrá perdón;
"viniéssem a vistas si oviesse dent sabor.
"Otros mandados ha en esta mi cort:
"Dí*da*go e Ferrando, los iffantes de Carrión,
"sabor han de casar con sus fijas amas a dos.
"Se*e*d buenos mensageros, e ruégovoslo yo
"que gelo digades al buen Campeador:
"abrá y ondra e creçrá en onor,
"por conssagrar con iffantes de Carrión."
Fabló Minaya e plogo a Per Vermu*doz:*
"Rogar gelo emos lo que dezides vos;
"después faga el Çid lo que oviere sabor."
"—Dezid a R*o*y Díaz, el que en buen ora na*çió,*
"quel iré a vistas do aguisado f*o*re;
"do el*le* dixiere, y sea el mojón.
"Andar le quiero a mio Çid en toda pro."
Espidiensse al rey, con esto tornados son,
van pora Valençia ellos e todos los sos.
Quando lo sopo el buen Campeador,
apriessa cavalga, a reçebirlos salió;
sonrrisós mio Çid e bien los abraçó:
"¡Venides, Minaya, e vos, Per Vermu*doz!*
"En pocas tierras a tales dos varones.
"¿Commo son las saludes de Alfons mio señor?
"¿si es pagado o reçibió el don?"

our honor will increase and we'll get ahead in the world."
They approached King Alfonso with that secret matter:
102. "We ask your favor as our king and lord;
if you consent, we wish to have you
request the Champion's daughters in our behalf;
we want to marry them for their honor and our benefit."
The king reflected and meditated for a long while;
"I exiled the good Champion,
and he has repaid the harm I did him with great benefits to me;
I don't know whether he will like this marriage;
but since you wish it, let's begin negotiations."
Minaya Álvar Fáñez and Pedro Bermúdez
were then summoned by the king,
who led them into a private room:
"Hear me, Minaya, and you, Pedro Bermúdez:
My Cid Ruy Díaz the Champion is serving me well,
he deserves to receive my pardon, and he will;
if he liked, we could have a formal meeting.
There are other matters relating to my court:
Diego and Fernando, the young lords of Carrión,
wish to marry his two daughters.
Be good messengers, I beg of you,
and report this to the good Champion:
he will gain honor thereby, and his wealth will increase,
if he forms a marriage alliance with the young lords of Carrión."
Minaya said, and Pedro Bermúdez agreed:
"We shall ask him about what you say;
then let the Cid do as he pleases."
"Tell Ruy Díaz, the man born in a lucky hour,
that I will go to meet him at any reasonable place;
let the venue be wherever he decides.
I want to favor My Cid in every way."
They took leave of the king, and returned;
they and all their men headed for Valencia.
When the good Champion learned of this,
he rode out quickly to meet them;
My Cid smiled and hugged them warmly:
"You have come, Minaya, and you, Pedro Bermúdez!
Very few lands possess two such men.
What news do you bring from my lord Alfonso?
Is he contented? Did he accept the gift?"

Dixo Minaya: "d' alma e de coraçón
"es pagado, e davos su amor."
Dixo mio Çid: "grado al Criador!"
Esto diziendo, conpieçan la razón,
lo quel rogava Alfons el de León
de dar sues fijas a ifantes de Carrión,
quel connosçie i ondra e creçrié en onor,
que gelo conssejava d' alma e de coraçón.
Quando lo oyó mio Çid el buen Campeador,
una gran ora penssó e comidió:
"Esto gradesco a Cristus el mio señor.
"Echado fu de tierra, he tollida la onor,
"con grand afán gané lo que he yo;
"a Dios lo gradesco que del rey he su *amor*,
"e pídenme mis fijas pora ifantes de Carrión.
"¿Dezid, Minaya e vos Per Vermudoz,
"d' aqueste casamiento que semeja a vos?"
"—Lo que a vos ploguiere esso dezimos nos."
Dixo el Çid: "de grand natura son ifantes de Carrión,
"ellos son mucho urgullosos e an part en la cort,
"deste casamiento non avría sabor;
"mas pues lo conseja el que más vale que nos,
"fablemos en ello, en la poridad seamos nos.
"Afé Dios del çielo que nos acuerde en lo mijor."
"—Con todo esto, a vos dixo Alfons
"que vos vernié a vistas do oviéssedes sabor;
"querer vos ye veer e darvos su amor,
"acordar vos yedes después a todo lo mejor."
Essora dixo el Çid: "plazme de coraçón."
"—Estas vistas o las ayades vos,"
dixo Minaya, "vos seed sabidor."
"—Non era maravilla si quisiesse el rey Alfons,
"fasta do lo fallássemos buscar lo iriemos nos,
"por darle grand ondra commo a rey *e señor*.
"Mas lo que él quisiere, esso queramos nos.
"Sobre Tajo, que es una agua *mayor*,
"ayamos vistas quando lo quiere mio señor."
Escrivien cartas, bien las seelló,
con dos cavalleros luego las enbió:
lo que el rey quisiere, esso ferá el Campeador.
103. Al rey ondrado delant le echaron las cartas;

Minaya said: "With heart and soul
he is contented, and he is restoring his favor to you."
My Cid said: "I thank the Creator!"
Saying this, they entered into the matter
of the request made by Alfonso, lord of León,
to marry his daughters to the young lords of Carrión,
which he knew to be to his honor and an advancement in wealth,
and which he advised him to do with heart and soul.
When My Cid the good Champion heard this,
he reflected and meditated a long while:
"For this I am grateful to Christ my Lord.
I was exiled, my property is confiscated,
with great toil I won what I now have;
I thank God that I have the king's favor,
and my daughters are requested for the young lords of Carrión.
Tell me, Minaya, and you, Pedro Bermúdez,
what do you think about this marriage?"
"We agree to anything that pleases you."
The Cid said: "The young lords of Carrión are of high lineage,
they are very haughty and are members of the royal court;
I don't like the idea of this marriage,
but since one more powerful than we are advises it,
let's discuss it, keeping it a secret.
May God in heaven lead us to make the best decision!"
"Besides all that, Alfonso sends word to you
that he'd meet you formally wherever you choose;
he'd like to see you and restore his favor to you;
after that, you'd come to the best possible terms."
The Cid then said: "I heartily concur."
"As to where that meeting will be held,"
Minaya said, "*you* are to judge."
"It would be natural, if King Alfonso wanted to meet,
for *us* to seek *him* out wherever he might be,
in order to give him great honor as our king and lord.
But let us agree to whatever he likes.
On the Tajo, which is a major river,
let us meet whenever my lord wishes."
He had a letter written, which he sealed firmly
and then sent off with two knights:
whatever the king wished, the Champion would do.
103. The letter was presented to the honored king;

quando las vío, de coraçón se paga:
"Saludadme a mio Çid, el que en buena çinxo espada;
"sean las vistas destas tres sedmanas;
"s' yo bivo so, allí iré sin falla."
Non lo detardan, a mio Çid se tornavan.
Della parte e della pora las vistas se adobavan;
¿quién vido por Castiella tanta mula preçiada,
e tanto palafré que bien anda,
cavallos gruessos e corredores sin falla,
tanto buen pendón meter en buenas astas,
escudos boclados con oro e con plata,
mantos e pielles e buenos çendales d' Alexándria?
Conduchos largos el rey enbiar mandava
a las aguas de Tajo, o las vistas son aparejadas.
Con el rey atantas buenas conpañas.
Iffantes de Carrión mucho alegres andan,
lo uno adebdan e lo otro pagavan;
commo ellos tenién, creçer les ýa la ganançia,
quantos quisiessen averes d' oro o de plata.
El rey don Alfonso a priessa cavalgava,
cuemdes e podestades e muy grandes mesnadas.
Ifantes de Carrión lievan grandes conpañas.
Con el rey van leoneses e mesnadas gallizianas,
non son en cuenta, sabet, las castellanas;
sueltan las riendas, a las vistas se van adeliñadas.

Grado al Criador e a vos, Çid, barba vellida!
odo lo que vos feches es de buena guisa.
Non serán menguadas en todos vuestros días!"
—Quando vos nos casáredes bien seremos ricas."

10. "—Mugier doña Ximena, grado al Criador.
A vos digo, mis fijas, don Elvira e doña Sol:
deste vuestro casamiento creçremos en onor;
mas bien sabet verdad que non lo levanté yo:
pedidas a vos ha e rogadas el mio señor Alfons,
atan firme mientre e de todo coraçón
que yo nulla cosa nol sope dezir de no.
Metivos en sus manos, fijas, amas ados;
bien me lo creades, que él vos casa, ca non yo."

11. Penssaron de adobar essora el palaçio,
por el suelo e suso tan bien encortinado,
tanta pórpola e tanto xámed e tanto paño preciado.
Sabor abriedes de seer e de comer en el palaçio.
Todos sos cavalleros apriessa son juntados.
Por iffantes de Carrión essora enbiaron,
cavalgan los iffantes, adelant adeliñavan al palaçio,
con buenas vestiduras e fuertemientre adobados;
de pie e a sabor, ¡Dios, qué quedos entraron!
Reçibiólos mio Çid, con todos sos vasallos;
a elle e a ssu mugier delant se le omillaron,
e ivan posar en un preçioso escaño.
Todos los de mio Çid tan bien son acordados,
están parando mientes al que en buen ora nasco.
El Campeador en pie es levantado:
¡Pues que a fazer lo avemos, por qué lo imos tardando?
¡Venit acá, Álbar Fáñez, el que yo quiero e amo!
affé amas mis fijas, métolas en vuestra mano;
sabedes que al rey assí gelo he mandado,
no lo quiero fallir por nada de quanto ay parado:
a ifantes de Carrión dadlas con vuestra mano,
e prendan bendiçiones e vayamos recabdando."
—Estoz dixo Minaya: "esto faré yo de grado."
Levántanse derechas e metiógelas en mano.
A ifantes de Carrión Minaya va fablando:
"Afevos delant Minaya, amos sodes hermanos.
Por mano del rey Alfons, que a mí lo ovo mandado,
dovos estas dueñas, —amas son fijas dalgo,—

when he saw it, he was pleased at heart:
"Greet My Cid for me, the man who girded on his sword in a lucky hour;
let the meeting be in three weeks from now;
if I'm alive, I'll go there without fail."
Without delay they returned to My Cid.
On both sides preparations were made for the meeting;
who had ever seen in Castile so many expensive mules,
so many easy-riding palfreys,
stout horses that were flawless runners,
so many fine pennants attached to fine lance shafts,
shields with bosses of gold and silver,
mantles, furs, and fine silk fabrics from Alexandria?[26]
The king had copious provisions sent
to the Tajo river, where the meeting was being arranged.
With the king went many fine troops.
The young lords of Carrión were very cheerful,
incurring debts for some items and paying for others;
they were sure that their wealth would increase,
and they'd have all the gold and silver they wanted.
King Alfonso rode swiftly,
with counts, barons, and very large companies of men.
The young lords of Carrión brought along numerous troops.
The king was accompanied by companies from León and Galicia;
I'll have you know that those from Castile couldn't be counted;
they gave their horses free rein, and set out for the rendezvous.

[SUMMARY of strophes **104–106** (verses **1985–2155**): The Cid sets out for the meeting with his chief vassals, leaving others to guard Valencia and his family. He arrives one day after the king, to whom he does homage in great humility. The king pardons him, and the young lords of Carrión greet him obsequiously. The next day, the Cid offers a banquet. The day after that, the king makes the formal request of the Cid to marry his daughters Elvira and Sol to the lords of Carrión; the Cid leaves the matter entirely in the hands of the king, who orders the marriage. The Cid is now to treat the bridegrooms as his own sons and take them to Valencia. Concurring, the Cid nevertheless reminds the king that this marriage was *his* doing; the brides will be given away not by him, but by Álvar Fáñez as the king's proxy.]

---

26. Recent editors read *Andria* ("Andros").

[Tiradas 107–114 (versos 2156–2337):]

107. Sobrel so cavallo Bavieca mio Çid salto d*io;*
"Aquí lo digo, ante mio señor el rey Alfons:
"qui quiere ir a las bodas, o reçebir mi*o* don,
"daquend vaya comigo; cuedo quel avrá pro."
Yas espidió mio Çid de so señor Alfons,
non quiere quel escurra, dessí luego*l* quitó.
Veriedes cavalleros, que bien andantes son,
besar las manos, espedirse de rey Alfons:
"Merçed vos sea e fazednos este perdón:
"hiremos en poder de mio Çid a Valençia la mayor;
"seremos a las bodas d' ifantes de Carrión
"he de fijas de mio Çid, de don Elvira e doña Sol."
Esto plogo al rey, e a todos los soltó;
la conpaña del Çid creçe, e la del rey mengó,
grandes son las yentes que van con el Canpeador.
Adeliñan pora Valençia, la que en buen punto ganó.
A Fernando e a Dí*a*go aguardar los mandó
a Per Vermu*doz* e Muño Gustioz,
—en casa de mio Çid non a dos mejores,
que sopiessen *sus* mañas d'infantes de Carrión.
E va i A*n*suor Gonçál*vez,* que era bullidor,
que es largo de lengua, mas en lo al non es tan pro.
Grant ondra les dan a ifantes de Carrión.
Afelos en Valençia, la que mio Çid gañó;
quando a ella assomaron, los gozos son mayores.
Dixo mio Çid a don Pero e a Muño Gustioz:
"Dad les un reyal a ifantes de Carrión,
"e vos con ellos se*ed,* que assí vos lo mando yo.
"Quando viniere la mañana, que apuntare el sol,
"verán a sus esposas, a don Elvira e a doña Sol."
108. Todos essa noch f*o*ron á sus posadas,
mio Çid el Campeador al alcáçer entrava;
reçibiólo doña Ximena e sus fijas amas:
"¿Venides, Campeador, buena çinxiestes espada?
"¡muchos dias vos veamos con los ojos de las caras!"
"—¡Grado al Criador, vengo, mugier ondrada!
"yernos vos adugo de que avremos ondrança;
"¡gradídmelo, mis fijas, ca bien vos he casadas!"
109. Besáronle las manos la mugier e las fijas
e todas las dueñas *de quien son servidas:*

107. My Cid leaped onto his horse Babieca;
"Here I say it, before my lord King Alfonso:
whoever wants to come to the wedding and receive my gift,
come with me right now; I believe it will be to his benefit."
Now My Cid took leave of his lord Alfonso;
he didn't want him to escort him, but left him on the very spot.
There you might see fortunate knights
kissing King Alfonso's hands and taking leave of him:
"May it be your will to grant us leave:
we shall go under My Cid's protection to the great city of Valencia;
we shall attend the wedding of the young lords of Carrión
and My Cid's daughters, Doña Elvira and Doña Sol."
The king consented, and gave everyone permission to go;
the Cid's party grew in numbers, while the king's decreased;
numerous were those who left with the Champion.
They headed for Valencia, which he had won at a propitious moment
As for Fernando and Diego, he ordered them to be watched
by Pedro Bermúdez and Muño Gustioz
(in the Cid's retinue there weren't two better men)
to learn the ways of the young lords of Carrión.
Also in the group was Ansur González, who was a loudmouth,
glib of tongue but not much good for anything else.
The young lords of Carrión were shown great honor.
Now they reached Valencia, which My Cid had conquered;
when they found themselves there, their joy increased.
My Cid said to Don Pedro and Muño Gustioz:
"Give the young lords of Carrión an apartment,
and stay with them; those are my orders.
When morning comes and the sun appears,
they will join their brides, Doña Elvira and Doña Sol."
108. Everyone went to his lodging for the night;
My Cid the Champion entered the citadel;
he was greeted by Doña Jimena and his two daughters:
"So you're back, Champion, with your good sword girded on?
May these eyes of ours behold you for many years!"
"Thanks to the Creator I'm back, my honored wife!
I bring you sons-in-law from whom we shall derive honor;
daughters, thank me, for I have found you good husbands!"
109. His hands were kissed by his wife and daughters
and all the ladies who waited on them:

"Thanks to the Creator and to you, Cid of the elegant beard!
Whatever you do is well done.
They will know no poverty as long as you live!"
"When you give us away, we will truly be noblewomen."
110. "My wife Doña Jimena, I thank the Creator.
To you, my daughters Doña Elvira and Doña Sol, I say
that we will gain in wealth from this marriage of yours;
but, to tell the truth, it wasn't I who broached the subject;
it was my lord Alfonso who requested and asked for you,
so firmly and warmly
that I was totally unable to refuse.
I placed both of you in his hands, my daughters;
believe me, *he* is giving you away, not I."
111. Now they began to adorn the palace
with fine carpets on the floors and walls,
and much purple, samite, and rare fabrics.
You would have been delighted to be in the palace and eat there.
All his knights assembled quickly.
Then the young lords of Carrión were sent for;
the young lords rode straight for the palace,
beautifully dressed and richly adorned;
what a pleasure it was to see them walk in so mannerfully!
My Cid and all his vassals welcomed them;
they bowed to him and his wife
and went to sit down on a costly bench.
All of My Cid's men were of one mind,
giving their attention to the man born in a lucky hour.
The Champion has stood up:
"Since it must be done, why are we putting it off?
Come here, Álvar Fáñez, whom I love and cherish!
Here are my two daughters, I place them in your hands;
you know that I promised this to the king;
I don't want to go back on all we agreed on for anything in the world:
give them with your own hand to the young lords of Carrión,
let them receive the blessings and let us perform the ceremony."
Then Minaya said: "I shall do so gladly."
The brides stood up and he handed them to him.
Minaya said, addressing the young lords of Carrión:
"Here you are, brothers both, before Minaya.
By the hand of King Alfonso, who ordered me to,
I give you these ladies, noblewomen both,

"que las tomassedes por mugieres a ondra e a recabdo."
Amos las reçiben d' amor e de grado,
a mio Çid e a su mugier van besar la mano.
Quando ovieron aquesto fecho, salieron del palacio,
pora Santa María a priessa adelinnando;
el obispo don Jerome vistiós tan privado,
a la puerta de la eclegia sediellos sperando;
dióles bendictiones, la missa a cantado.
Al salir de la ecclegia cavalgaron tan privado,
a la glera de Valençia fuera dieron salto;
¡Dios, qué bien tovieron armas el Çid e sos vasallos!
Tres cavallos cameó el que en buen ora nasco.
Mio Çid de lo que vidié mucho era pagado:
ifantes de Carrión bien an cavalgado.
Tórnanse con las dueñas, a Valençia an entrado;
ricas fueron las bodas en el alcáçer ondrado,
e al otro día fizo mio Çid fincar siete tablados:
antes que entrassen a yantar todos los crebantaron.
Quinze días conplidos en las bodas duraron,
çerca de los quinze días yas van los fijos dalgo.
Mio Çid don Rodrigo, el que en buen ora nasco,
entre palafrés e mulas e corredores cavallos,
en bestias sines al çiento ha mandados;
mantos e pelliçones e otros vestidos largos;
non foron en cuenta los averes monedados.
Los vassallos de mio Çid, assí son acordados,
cada uno por sí sos dones avién dados.
Qui aver quiere prender bien era abastado;
ricos tornan a Castiella los que a las bodas llegaron.
Yas ivan partiendo aquestos ospedados,
espidiéndos de Roy Díaz, el que en buen ora nasco,
e a todas las dueñas e a los fijos dalgo;
por pagados se parten de mio Çid e de sos vassallos.
Grant bien dizen dellos ca será aguisado.
Mucho eran alegres Dídago e Ferrando;
estos foron fijos del comde don Gonçalvo.
Venidos son a Castiella aquestos ospedados,
el Çid e sos hyernos en Valençia son rastados.
Y moran los ifantes bien cerca de dos años,
los amores que les fazen mucho eran sobejanos.
Alegre era el Çid e todos sos vassallos.

to take as your honored and legitimate wives."
They both received them lovingly and happily,
and kissed the hand of My Cid and his wife.
After this had taken place, they left the palace
and quickly went to Santa María;
Bishop Jérôme had dressed quickly
and was awaiting them at the church door;
he gave them his blessing and sang mass.
Upon leaving church they rode swiftly
out to the Valencia parade grounds;
What great feats of arms the Cid and his vassals performed!
He that was born in a lucky hour changed horses three times.
My Cid was very contented with what he saw:
the young lords of Carrión rode well.
They and the ladies returned, entering Valencia;
the wedding party in the honorable citadel was delightful,
and the next day the Cid had seven *tablados* erected:
before going in to lunch, they had toppled them all.
The wedding celebrations lasted fifteen full days,
after the fifteen days the noblemen departed.
My Cid Don Rodrigo, he that was born in a lucky hour,
what with palfreys, mules, and swift horses,
gave away a hundred mounts, not counting everything else;
mantles, pelisses, and other full-length garments;
the coined money was beyond calculation.
My Cid's vassals, all of one mind,
had each given presents.
Whoever wanted to take goods was well supplied with them;
those who had attended the wedding returned to Castile rich men.
Now those guests were departing,
taking leave of Ruy Díaz, the man born in a lucky hour,
and of all the ladies and noblemen;
they parted contentedly from My Cid and his vassals.
They had much good to say of them, as was only proper.
Diego and Fernando were very happy
(they were sons of Count Gonzalo).
Those guests arrived back in Castile;
the Cid and his sons-in-law remained in Valencia.
The young lords dwelt there for nearly two years,
being treated with unusual affection.
The Cid and all his vassals were happy.

¡Plega a santa María e al Padre santo
ques pague des casamiento mio Çid o el que lo ovo âlgo!
Las coplas deste cantar aquis van acabando.
El Criador vos vala con todos los sos santos.
112. En Valençia se*dí* mio Çid con todos *los sos,*
con e*ll*e amos *s*os yernos ifantes de Carrión.
Yaziés en un escaño, durmié el Campeador,
mala sobrevienta, sabed, que les cuntió:
saliós de la red e desatós el león.
En grant miedo se vieron por medio de la cort;
e*n*braçan los mantos los del Campeador,
e çercan el escaño, e fincan sobre so señor.
Ferran*t* Gonçál*v*ez, *ifant de Carrión,*
non vi*d*o allí dos alçasse, nin cámara abierta nin torre;
metiós sol esçaño, tanto ovo el pavor.
Dí*ag* Gonçál*v*ez por la puerta salió,
diziendo de la boca: "¡non veré Carrión!"
Tras una viga lagar metiós con grant pavor;
el manto e el brial todo suzio lo sacó.
En esto despertó el que en buen ora naçió;
vi*d*o çercado el escaño de *s*os buenos varones:
"¿Qués esto, mesnadas, o qué queredes vos?"
"—Ya señor ondrado, rebata nos dió el león."
Mio Çid fincó el cobdo, en pie se levantó,
el manto trae al cuello, e adeliñó pora' león;
el león quando lo vío, assí e*n*vergonçó,
ante mio Çid la cabeça premió e el rostro fincó.
Mio Çid don Rodrigo al cuello lo tomó,
e liévalo adestrando, en la red le metió.
A maravilla lo han quantos que i son,
e tornáronse al palaçio pora la cort.
Mio Çid por sos yernos demandó e no los falló;
maguer los están llamando, ninguno non responde.
Quando los fallaron, assí vinieron sin color;
non vi*di*estes tal juego commo iva por la cort;
mandólo vedar mio Çid el Campeador.
Muchos tovieron por enbaídos infantes de Carrión,
fiera cosa les pesa desto que les cuntió.

May it please the Blessed Virgin and the heavenly Father
that My Cid, and the king he esteems, derive joy from the marriage!
The strophes of this canto end here.
May the Creator and all his saints protect you![27]
112. My Cid and all his men dwelt in Valencia;
with him were his two sons-in-law, the young lords of Carrión.
The Champion was lying on a bench asleep
when, as I shall tell, they received an unpleasant jolt:
the lion which the Cid kept escaped from its cage.
Those in the great hall were in a fearful situation;
the Champion's men protected their arms with their capes,
surrounded their master's bench, and bent over him.
Fernán González, young lord of Carrión,
saw no place to retreat to, neither an open room nor a tower;
he hid under the bench, his fear was so great.
Diego González went out the door,
saying: "I'll never see Carrión again!"
In great dread, he hid behind the beam of a wine press;
when he came out, his cape and tunic were all soiled.
At that moment the man born in a lucky hour awoke;
he found his bench surrounded by his loyal men:
"What's going on, soldiers, what do you want?"
"O honored lord, the lion gave us a scare."
My Cid sat up, leaning on his elbow, then rose to his feet;
his cape behind his back, he headed for the lion;
when the lion saw him, it was so cowed
that it bowed its head and lowered its muzzle in the Cid's presence.
My Cid Don Rodrigo took it by the neck
and guided it back to its cage, shutting it in.
All who were present were amazed,
and returned to the great hall of the palace.
My Cid inquired after his sons-in-law, who couldn't be found;
though they were called for, neither one responded.
When they were found, they were quite pale;
you've never heard such jokes as were circulated through the hall;
My Cid the Champion ordered a stop to them.
The young lords of Carrión considered themselves gravely offended,
they were mortally grieved by what had befallen them.

---

27. For reasons obvious from the text, most editions begin a new subdivision here
("*cantar tercero*").

113. Ellos en esto estando, don avién grant pesar,
fuerças de Marruecos Valençia vienen çercar;
en el campo de Quarto ellos fueron posar,
cinquaenta mill tiendas fincadas ha de las cabdales;
aqueste era el rey Búcar, sil oviestes contar.
114. Alegravas el Çid e todos *sos* varones,
que les creçe la ganançia, grado al Criador.
Mas, sabed, de cuer les pesa a ifantes de Carrión;
ca veyén tantas tiendas de moros de que non avié*n* sabor,
Amos hermanos a part salidos son:
"Catamos la ganançia e la pérdida no;
"ya en esta batalla a entrar abremos nos;
"esto es aguisado por non ve*e*r Carrión,
"bibdas remandrán fijas del Campeador."
Oyó la poridad aquel Muño Gustioz,
vino con estas nuevas a mio Çid el Campeador:
"Evades vuestros yernos tan osados so*n*,
"por entrar en batalla desean Carrión.
"Idlos conortar, sí vos vala el Criador,
"que sean en paz e non ayan i raçión.
"Nos con vusco la vençremos, e valer nos ha el Criador."
Mio Çid don Rodrigo sonrrisando salió:
"Dios vos salve, yernos, ifantes de Carrión,
"en braços tenedes mis fijas ¡tan blancas commo el sol!
"Yo desseo lides, e vos a Carrión,
"en Valençia folgad a todo vuestro sabor,
"ca d' aquellos moros yo so sabidor;
"arrancar me los trevo con la merçed del Criador."

113. While they were in that situation, which vexed them greatly,
Moroccan forces came to besiege Valencia;
they encamped in the field of Cuarto,
pitching fifty thousand rich tents;
it was General Búcar, if you've ever heard of him.
114. The Cid and all his men were delighted
because they would win more booty, thanks to the Creator.
But I'll have you know, the young lords of Carrión were sad at heart,
seeing so many Moorish tents, which was not to their liking.
The two brothers conferred in private:
"We had calculated on gains, not losses;
now we will have to participate in this battle;
it's a sure thing we'll never see Carrión again;
the Champion's daughters will be widows."
That Muño Gustioz overheard the private conversation,
and reported it to My Cid the Champion:
"See here, your sons-in-law are so brave
that they'd rather be in Carrión than in battle.
Go and comfort them (so may the Creator keep you!)
so they will be in peace and take no share in the fight.
You and we will win it, and the Creator will protect us."
My Cid Don Rodrigo went out smiling:
"God save you, sons-in-law, young lords of Carrión;
you have recently wed my daughters, who are as bright as the sun!
I yearn for battle, and you for Carrión;
relax in Valencia to your heart's content,
because I know my way around those Moors;
I will venture to beat them with the help of the Creator."

[SUMMARY of strophes **115 & 116** (verses 2338–2382): (At this point, another MS sheet—about 50 lines—is missing. Apparently, the young lords insisted on fighting, and even on leading the charge, but Fernando ran away when attacked by a Moor. Pedro Bermúdez killed the Moor for him, generously giving him the credit and promising not to reveal the secret.) The Cid is pleased by the false report, but Pedro refuses the Cid's order to keep watching over the brothers. Álvar Fáñez expresses confidence in victory. Bishop Jérôme asks the Cid's permission to attack the Moors.]

[Tiradas 117–131 (versos 2383–2862):**]**

117. El obispo don Jer*om*e priso a espolonada
e ívalos ferir a cabo del albergada.
Por la su ventura e Dios quel amava
a los primeros colpes dos moros matava.
El astil a *cre*bado e metió mano al espada.
¡Ensayavas el obispo, Dios, qué bien lidiava!
Dos mató con lança e çinco con el espada.
Moros son muchos, derredor le çercavan,
dávanle grandes colpes, mas nol falssan las armas.
El que en buen ora nasco los ojos le fincava,
enbraçó el escudo e abaxó el asta,
aguijó a Bavieca, el cavallo que bien anda,
ívalos ferir de coraçón e de alma.
En las azes primeras el Campeador entrava,
abatió a siete e a quatro matava.
Plogo a Dios, aquesta *fo* el arrancada.
Mio Çid con los *s*os ca*d*e en alcança;
veriedes *cre*bar ta*n*tas cuerdas e arrancarse las estacas
e acostarse los tendales, con huebras eran tantas.
Los de mio Çid a los de Búcar de las tiendas los sacan.
118. Sácanlos de las tiendas, cáenlos en alcaz;
tanto braço con loriga veriedes caer a part,
tantas cabeças con yelmos que por el campo ca*d*en,
cavallos sin dueños salir a todas partes.
Siete migeros conplidos duró el segudar.
Mio Çid al rey Búcar ca*d*ió*l* en alcaz:
"¡Acá torna, Búcar! venist dalent mar.
"Ve*e*rte as con el Çid, el de la barba grant,
"saludar nos hemos amos, e tajaremos amizta*t*."
Respuso Búcar al Çid: "¡cofonda Dios tal amiztad!
"Espada tienes en mano e veot aguijar;
"así commo semeja, en mi la quieres ensayar.
"Mas si el cavallo non estropieça o conmigo non ca*d*e,
"non te juntarás conmigo fata dentro en la mar."
Aquí respuso mio Çid: "esto non será verdad."
Buen cavallo tiene Búcar e grandes saltos faz,
mas Bavieca el de mio Çid alcançándolo va.
Alcançólo el Çid a Búcar a tres braças del mar,
arriba alçó Colada, un grant colpe dádol ha,
las carbonclas del yelmo tollidas gelas ha,

[**Strophes 117–131** (verses 2383–2862):]

117. Bishop Jérôme spurred his horse onward
and attacked them at the edge of their camp.
Because of his own good luck and God's love for him,
he killed two Moors with his first blows.
Having broken his lance shaft, he took up his sword.
How the bishop strove, how well he fought!
He killed two with his lance and five with his sword.
The Moors were numerous and surrounded him;
they dealt him heavy blows but failed to pierce his armor.
The man born in a lucky hour had his eyes glued to him;
gripping his shield and lowering his lance,
he spurred Babieca, his swift steed,
and charged with heart and soul.
The Champion rode into the foremost ranks,
unhorsing seven and killing four.
It pleased God to make that action the victorious one.
My Cid and his men began the pursuit;
there you might see many tent cords broken and stakes pulled up
and tent poles knocked over, with all their many ornaments.
My Cid's men chased Búcar's men out of their tents.
118. They drove them from their tents and lit out in pursuit of them;
there you might see many a mail-clad arm flying off severed,
many a helmeted head falling to the ground,
riderless horses escaping in every direction.
The chase went on for seven full miles.
My Cid was pursuing General Búcar:
"Come back here, Búcar, you that came from across the sea!
You have to settle up with the Cid, the man with the long beard;
we must greet each other and pledge friendship."
Búcar answered the Cid: "May God confound such friendship!
You're brandishing a sword and I see you hastening after me;
it looks to me as if you wanted to try it out on *me*.
But if my horse doesn't stumble and fall with me,
you won't overtake me before I'm in the sea."
Then My Cid replied: "Not so!"
Búcar had a good horse, which was moving at full gallop,
but My Cid's Babieca was catching up with him.
The Cid overtook Búcar six meters into the sea;
he lifted up Colada and dealt him a great blow,
making the garnets spring out of his helmet;

cortól el yelmo e, librado todo lo al,
fata la çintura el espada llegado ha.
Mató a Búcar, al rey de allén mar,
e ganó a Tizón que mill marcos d' oro val.
Vençió la batalla maravillosa e grant,
Aquís ondró mio Çid e quantos con el*le* están.
119. Con estas gananças yas ivan tornando;
sabet, todos de firme robavan el campo.
A las tiendas eran llegados *con* el que en buen*a* nasco,
Mio Çid R*o*y Diaz, el Campeador contado,
con dos espadas que él preçiava algo
por la matança vinía tan privado,
la cara fronzida e almófar soltado,
cofia sobre los pelos fronzida della yaquanto.
De todas partes sos vassallos van llegando;
algo vi*di*é mio Çid de lo que era pagado,
alçó sos ojos, est*a*va adelant catando,
e vi*do* venir a Dí*a*go e a Fernando;
amos son fijos del co*m*de don Gonçal*v*o.
Alegrós mio Çid fermoso sonrrisando:
"¿Venides, mios yernos, mios fijos sodes amos?
"Sé que de lidiar bien sodes pagados;
"a Carrión de vos irán buenos mandados,
"cómmo al rey Búcar avemos arrancado.
"Commo yo fio por Dios y en todos los sos santos,
"desta arrancada nos iremos pagados."
Minaya Álbar Fáñez essora es llegado,
el escudo trae al cuello e todo espad*a*do;
de los colpes de las lanças non avié recabdo;
aquellos que gelos dieran non gelo avién logrado.
Por el cobdo ayuso la sangre destellando;
de veínte arriba ha moros matado;
"Grado a Dios e al padre que está en alto,
"e a vos, Çid, ¡que en buen ora f*o*stes nado!
"Matastes a Búcar e arrancamos el canpo.
"Todos estos bienes de vos son e de vuestros vassallos.
"E vuestros yernos aquí son ensayados,
"fartos de lidiar con moros en el campo."
Dixo mio Çid: "yo desto so pagado;

he cut through the helmet and ripped through everything else,
driving his sword to his waist.
He killed Búcar, the general from overseas,
and won Tizona,[28] which was worth a thousand marks of gold.
He won that marvelous, great battle.
Here My Cid and all who were with him honored themselves.
119. Now they were returning with the spoils;
I'll have you know they were all sedulously plundering the camp.
They reached the tents along with the man born in a lucky hour;
My Cid Ruy Díaz, the renowned Champion,
with two swords that he esteemed highly,
rode swiftly through the scene of slaughter,
his face furrowed, his hood of mail hanging loose,
the cloth cap on his hair somewhat wrinkled.
His vassals arrived from every direction;
My Cid saw something that gladdened him;
raising his eyes and looking straight ahead,
he saw coming Diego and Fernando,
the two sons of Count Gonzalo.
My Cid, happy, gave a lovely smile:
"You're back, sons-in-law, you that are my sons?
I know that you are well contented to fight;
a good report about you will be sent to Carrión,
telling of how we vanquished General Búcar.
As I trust in God and all his saints,
we will derive pleasure from this victory."
Then Minaya Álvar Fáñez arrived,
his shield slung from his neck, sword marks all over it;
he wasn't concerned about the lance thrusts;
those he had received hadn't harmed him.
Enemy blood was flowing down his elbow;
he had killed over twenty Moors;
"I thank God the Father in heaven,
and you, Cid, who were born in a lucky hour!
You killed Búcar and we won the field.
All this booty belongs to you and your vassals.
And your sons-in-law here have been tested;
they have had their fill of combating Moors."
My Cid said: "I am pleased by that;

---

28. The Cid's second legendary sword; its name is thought to mean "blazing."

"quando agora son buenos, adelant serán preçiados."
Por bien lo dixo el Çid mas ellos lo touieron a *escarnio*.
Todos *lo*s gana*do*s a Valencia son llega*do*s;
alegre es mio Çid con todos *so*s *vassallos,*
que a la raçión ca*dié* de plata seys çientos marcos.
Los yernos de mio Çid quando este aver tomaron
desta arrancada, que lo tenién en so salvo,
cuydaron que en *so*s días nunqua serién minguados.
F*o*ron en Valençia muy bien arreados,
conduchos a sazones, buenas pieles e buenos mantos.
Mucho son alegres mio Çid e *so*s vassallos.
120. Grant f*o* el día *p*or la cort del Campeador,
después que esta batalla vencieron e al rey Búcar mató,
alçó la mano, a la barba se tomó:
"Grado a Cristus, que del mundo es señor,
"quando veo lo que avía sabor,
"que lidiaran comigo en campo mios yernos amos a dos;
"mandados buenos irán dellos a Carrión,
"commo son ondrados e aver *nos han* grant pro."
121. Sobejanas son las ganançias que todos an ganad*o*;
lo uno es *dellos,* lo otro han en salvo.
Mandó mio Çid, el que en buen ora nasco,
desta batalla que han arrancado
que todos prisiessen so derecho contado,
e *el so* quint*o de mio* Çid non fosse olbidado.
Assí lo fazen todos, ca eran acordados.
Ca*dié*ronle en quinta al Çid seys çientos cavallos,
e otras azémilas e camellos largos
tantos son de muchos que non serién contados.
122. Todas estas ganançias fizo el Canpeador.
"¡Grado ha Dios que del mundo es señor!
"Antes fu minguado, agora rico so,
"que he aver e tierra e oro e onor,
"e son mios yernos ifantes de Carrión;
"arranco las lides commo plaze al Criador,
"moros e cristianos de mí han grant pavor.
"Allá dentro en Marruecos, o las mezquitas son,
"que abrám de mi salto quiçab alguna noch
"ellos lo temen, ca non lo pie*n*sso yo:
"no los iré buscar, en Valençia seré yo,
"ellos me darán parias con ayuda del Criador,

if they are good men now, in the future they will be famous."
The Cid said that kindly, but they took it as mockery.
All the spoils arrived in Valencia;
My Cid and all his vassals were happy,
for each one's share was worth six hundred marks of silver.
When My Cid's sons-in-law took that wealth
won in the victory and stored it away,
they thought they would never be in want as long as they lived.
They were well equipped in Valencia,
with the finest food, good furs, and good mantles.
My Cid and his vassals were very happy.

120. It was a great day in the Champion's hall
after they won that battle and he killed General Búcar;
he raised his hand and clutched his beard:
"I thank Christ, who is Lord of the world,
since I have seen what pleased me,
both my sons-in-law fighting by my side in the field;
good reports of them will be sent to Carrión,
telling of their honor and how they will be of great benefit to us."

121. Numerous were the spoils everybody won;
part of it belonged to the Cid's men, the rest was kept by the young lords.
My Cid, he that was born in a lucky hour, gave orders
that from the battle they had won
each man was to take exactly what was due him,
and that My Cid's fifth part was not to be forgotten.
And they all did so, for they were in agreement.
As part of his fifth the Cid received six hundred horses,
and the other beasts of burden and numerous camels
were so abundant they couldn't be counted.

122. All those gains were made by the Champion.
"Thanks to God, who is Lord of the world!
I was once needy, now I am rich,
owning goods and land and gold and wealth,
and my sons-in-law are young lords of Carrión;
I win battles as it pleases the Creator,
both Moors and Christians are greatly afraid of me.
Down there in Morocco, where the mosques are,
they fear I may perhaps attack them some night,
even though I have no such intention:
I won't go after them, I'll remain in Valencia
and, with the Creator's help, they'll pay me tribute,

"que paguen a mí o a qui yo ovier sabor."
Grandes son los gozos en Valençia *la mayor*
de todas sus conpañas *de* mio Çid el Canpeador,
d' aquesta arrancada que lidiaron de coraçón;
grandes son los gozos de *sos* yernos amos a dos:
valía de çinco mill marcos ganaron amos a dos;
muchos tienen por ricos ifantes de Carrión.
Ellos con los otros vinieron a la cort;
aquí está con mio Çid el obispo do Jer*o*me,
el bueno de Álbar Fáñez, cavallero lidiador,
e otros muchos que crió el Campeador;
quando entraron ifantes de Carrión,
recibiólos Minaya por mio Çid el Campeador:
"Acá venid, cuñados, que mas valemos por vos."
Assí commo llegaron, pagós el Campeador:
"Evades aquí, yernos, la mi*e* mugier de pro,
"e amas la*s* mis fijas, don Elvira e doña Sol;
"bien vos abraçen e sírvanvos de coraçón.
"¡Grado a santa María, madre del nuestro señor Dios!
"destos *v*uestros casamientos vos abredes honor.
"Buenos mandados irán a tierras de Carrión."
123. A estas palabras fabló *ifant* Ferran*do:*
"Grado al Criador e a vos, Çid ondrado,
"tantos avemos de averes que no son contados;
"por vos avemos ondra e avemos lidiado,
"vençiemos moros en campo e matamos
"a aquel rey Búcar, traydor provado.
"Pensad de lo otro, que lo nuestro tenémoslo en saluo."
Vassallos de mio Çid se*d*iense sonrrisando:
quien lidiara mejor o quien fora en alcanço;
mas non fallavan i a Dí*d*ago ni a Ferrando.
Por aquestos juegos que ivan levantando,
elas noches e los días tan mal los escarmentando,
tal mal se conssejaron estos iffantes amos.
Amos salieron a part, veramientre son hermanos;
desto que ellos fablaron nos parte non ayamos;
"—Vayamos pora Carrión, aquí mucho detardamos.
"Los averes que tenemos grandes son e sobejanos,
"despender no los podremos mientra que *bivos seamos.*
124. "—Pidamos nuestras mugieres al Çid Campeador,
"digamos que las llevaremos a tierras de Carrión,

either to me or to whomever I feel like appointing."
Great was the joy in mighty Valencia
felt by all the troops of My Cid the Champion
because of that victory they had won courageously;
great was the joy of his two sons-in-law:
the two had gained booty worth five thousand marks;
the young lords of Carrión considered themselves very wealthy.
They and the others assembled in the great hall;
there with My Cid was Bishop Jérôme,
the good Álvar Fáñez, a knight strong in battle,
and many others whom the Champion had reared;
when the young lords of Carrión came in,
Minaya greeted them in behalf of My Cid the Champion:
"Come here, kinsmen, for you have made us more powerful."
As soon as they arrived, the Champion was pleased:
"Sons-in-law, here you see my excellent wife
and my two daughters, Doña Elvira and Doña Sol;
let them hug you warmly and serve you gladly.
I thank the Blessed Virgin, mother of our Lord God!
You shall benefit by these marriages of yours.
Good reports will be sent to the lands of Carrión."
123. These words were answered by young lord Fernando:
"I thank the Creator and you, honored Cid;
we have so many possessions they can't be counted;
through you we are honored and we have fought,
conquering Moors in the field and slaying
that General Búcar, a proven traitor.
You worry about the rest, for we have our property in safe storage."
My Cid's vassals were smiling:
they discussed who had fought best and who had taken part in the pursuit,
but they hadn't discovered Diego or Fernando in either group.
Because of the jokes they kept telling,
mocking them harshly both night and day,
those two young lords contrived an evil plan.
The two of them, true brothers, conferred in secret;
let us not associate ourselves with what they said:
"Let's return to Carrión, we've tarried here too long.
Our possessions are great and numerous,
we couldn't spend it all no matter how long we live.
124. Let's ask the Cid Champion for our wives,
let's say we're taking them to the lands of Carrión,

"enseñar las hemos do *e*llas heredad*a*s son.
"Sacar las hemos de Valençia, de poder del Campeador;
"después en la carrera feremos nuestro sabor,
"ante que nos retrayan lo que cuntió del león.
"¡Nos de natura somos de co*m*des de Carrión!
"Averes levaremos grandes que valen grant valor;
"escarniremos las fijas del Canpeador."
"—D' aquestos averes sienpre seremos ricos omnes,
"podremos casar con fijas de reyes o de enperadores
"ca de natura somos de co*m*des de Carrión.
"Assí las escarniremos a fijas del Campeador,
"antes que nos retrayan lo que *fo* del león."
Con aqueste conssejo amos tornados son,
fabló Ferrán*t* Gonçál*v*ez e fizo callar la cort:
"¡Sí vos vala el Criador, Çid Campeador!
"que plega a doña Ximena e primero a vos
"e a Minaya Álbar Fáñez e a quantos aquí son:
"dadnos nuestras mugieres que avemos a bendiçiones;
"levar las hemos a nuestras tierras de Carrión,
"meter las hemos en arras que les diemos por onores;
"verán vuestras fijas lo que avemos nos,
"los fijos que oviéremos en qué avrán partiçión."
Nos curiava de *fonta mio* Çid el Campeador;
"Darvos he mis fijas e algo de lo mio;
"vos les diestes villas por arras en tierras de Carrión,
"yo quiéroles dar axuvar tres mill marcos de *valor;*
"darvos e mulas e palafrés, muy gruessos de sazón,
"cavallos pora en diestro fuertes e corredores,
"e muchas vestiduras de paños e de çiclatones;
"darvos he dos espadas, a Colada e a Tizón,
"bien lo sabedes vos que las gané a guisa de varón;
"mios fijos sodes amos, quando mis fijas vos do;
"allá me levades las telas del coraçón.
"Que lo sepan en Gallizia e en Castiella e en León,
"con que riqueza enbío mios yernos amos a dos.
"A mis fijas sirvades, que vuestras mugieres son;
"si bien las servides, yo vos rendré buen galardón."
Atorgado lo han esto iffantes de Carrión.
Aquí reçiben fijas del Campeador;
conpieçan a reçebir lo que el Çid mandó.
Quando son pagados a todo so sabor,

letting them be seen where they have gained estates.
We must remove them from Valencia and the Champion's power;
later, on the journey, we shall do our will,
before they reproach us for that incident with the lion.
We are of the lineage of the counts of Carrión!
We'll take along great spoils that are extremely valuable;
we shall put to shame the daughters of the Champion."
"With those goods we will always be rich and noble;
we'll be able to marry daughters of kings or emperors,
for we are of the lineage of the counts of Carrión.
Thus we shall put to shame the daughters of the Champion,
before they reproach us with that story about the lion."
After hatching that plan they both returned;
Fernán González spoke, bidding those in the great hall be silent:
"So may the Creator keep you, Cid Champion!
May it please Doña Jimena and you above all
and Minaya Álvar Fáñez and all assembled here:
give us our lawfully wedded wives;
we shall take them to our lands in Carrión,
we shall settle them on the bride-gift estates we bestowed on them;
your daughters will see what we possess
and what our eventual children will share in."
My Cid the Champion suspected no affront;
"I shall give you my daughters and some of what I own;
you gave them estates as bride gifts in the lands of Carrión,
I shall give them a dowry worth three thousand marks;
I shall give you mules and palfreys, sturdy and fine,
as well as strong, swift chargers
and many garments of wool and of silk brocade;
I shall give you the two swords Colada and Tizona,
which, as you well know, I won by manly actions;
you are both my sons, since I give you my daughters;
with them you are taking away my heartstrings.
Let those in Galicia, Castile, and León know
with what wealth I am sending off my two sons-in-law.
Take care of my daughters, who are your wives;
if you take good care of them, I shall reward you well."
The young lords of Carrión consented to that.
Then they received the Champion's daughters,
and began receiving what the Cid had ordered them given.
When they were completely satisfied,

ya mandavan cargar iffantes de Carrión.
Grandes son las nuevas por Valençia la mayor.
Todos prenden armas e cavalgan a vigor,
por que escurren fijas del *Cid* a tierras de Carrión.
Ya quieren cavalgar, en espidimiento son.
Amas hermanas, don Elvira e doña Sol,
fincaron los inojos antel Çid Campeador:
"¡Merçed vos pedimos, padre, sí vos vala el Criador!
"vos nos engendrastes, nuestra madre nos parió;
"delant sodes amos, señora e señor.
"Agora nos enviades a tierras de Carrión,
"debdo nos es a cunplir lo que mandáredes vos.
"Assí vos pedimos merçed nos amas a dos,
"que ayades vuestros menssajes en tierras de Carrión."
Abraçólas mio Çid e saludólas amas a dos.
125. El*le* fizo aquesto, la madre lo doblava;
"¡Andad, fijas; d' aquí el Criador vos vala!
"de mí e de vuestro padre, bien avedes nuestra graçia.
"Id a Carrión do sodes heredadas,
"assí commo yo tengo, bien vos he casadas."
Al padre e a la madre las manos les besavan;
amos la bendixieron e diéronles su graçia.
Mio Çid e los otros de cavalgar penssavan,
a grandes guarnimientos, a cavallos e armas.
Ya salién los ifantes de Valençia la clara,
espi*di*éndos de las dueñas e de todas su*es* compañas.
Por la huerta de Valencia teniendo salién armas;
alegre va mio Çid con todas su*es* compañas.
Víolo en los avueros el que en buen*a* cinxo espada,
que estos casamientos non serién sin alguna tacha.
Nos puede repentir, que casadas las ha amas.
126. "¿O eres, mio sobrino, tú Félez Muñoz,
"primo eres de mis fijas amas d'alma e de coraçón?
"Mándot que vayas con ellas fata dentro en Carrión,
"verás las heredades que a mis fijas dadas son;
"con aquestas nuevas vernás al Campeador."
Dixo Félez Muñoz: "plazme d'alma e de coraçón."
Minaya Álbar Fáñez ante mio Çid se paró:
"Tornémosnos, Çid, a Valençia la mayor;
"que si a Dios ploguiere e al Padre Criador,
"ir las hemos ve*de*r a tierras de Carrión."

the young lords of Carrión had everything loaded.
Great was the activity throughout mighty Valencia.
Everyone took up arms and rode swiftly
to escort the Cid's daughters to the lands of Carrión.
They were about to ride off, they were taking their leave.
The two sisters, Doña Elvira and Doña Sol,
knelt down before the Cid and Champion:
"We ask your favor, father (so may the Creator keep you!).
You begot us, our mother gave birth to us;
you both stand before us, lady and lord.
Now you are sending us to the lands of Carrión;
it is our filial duty to comply with your orders.
Thus we both ask for a favor from you:
to keep sending messengers to the lands of Carrión."
My Cid embraced and kissed them both.
125. He did this, and their mother did twice as much:
"Go, daughters; from now on may the Creator protect you!
You are securely in our good graces, your father's and mine.
Go to Carrión, where you have estates;
it seems to me that I have given you good husbands."
They kissed their father's and mother's hands;
their two parents gave them their blessing and their favor.
My Cid and the others began to ride out
with fine trappings, steeds, and weapons.
Now the young lords left renowned Valencia,
taking leave of the ladies and all the soldiers.
They rode to the fertile Valencia plain, indulging in military sports;
My Cid and all his troops were happy.
The man who girded on his sword in a lucky hour saw by the omens
that those marriages wouldn't be without blemish.
He couldn't retract what he had done, for he had married off the two girls.
126. "Where are you, nephew Félez Muñoz,
loving cousin of my two daughters?
I order you to accompany them all the way to Carrión;
you'll see the estates that have been given to my daughters;
with that report you will return to the Champion."
Félez Muñoz said: "Yes, with my heart and soul."
Minaya Álvar Fáñez appeared before My Cid:
"Cid, let's go back to mighty Valencia;
for if it pleases God, our Father and Creator,
we shall visit them in the lands of Carrión."

"—A Dios vos acomendamos, don Elvira e doña Sol;
"atales cosas fed que en plazer caya a nos."
Respondién los yernos: "¡assí lo mande Dios!"
Grandes fueron los duelos a la departiçión.
El padre con las fijas lloran de coraçón,
assí fazían los cavalleros del Campeador.
"¡Oyas, sobrino, tú, Félez Muñoz!
"por Molina iredes, i yazredes una noch;
"saludad a mio amigo el moro Abengalvón:
"reçiba a mios yernos commo elle pudier mejor;
"dil que enbío mis fijas a tierras de Carrión,
"de lo que ovieren huebos sírvalas a so sabor,
"desí escúrralas fasta Medina por la mi amor.
"De quanto él fiziere yol daré por ello buen galardón."
Quomo la uña de la carne ellos partidos son.
Yas tornó pora Valençia el que en buen ora nasçió.
Piénssanse de ir ifantes de Carrión;
por Santa María d' Alvarrazín la posada *fecha fo,*
aguijan quanto pueden ifantes de Carrión;
felos en Molina con el moro Abengalvón.
El moro quando lo sopo, plógol de coraçón;
saliólos recebir con grandes avorozes;
¡Dios, que bien los sirvió a todo so sabor!
Otro día mañana con ellos cavalgó,
con dozientos cavalleros escurrir los mandó;
ivan troçir los montes, los que dizen de Luzón,
troçieron Arbuxuelo e llegaron a Salón,
o dizen el Anssarera ellos posados son.
A las fijas del Çid el moro sus donas dió,
buenos seños cavalos a ifantes de Carrión;
tod esto les fizo el moro por el amor del Çid Campeador.
Ellos vedién la riqueza que el moro sacó,
entramos hermanos conssejaron traçión:
"Ya pues que a dexar avemos fijas del Campeador,
"si pudiéssemos matar el moro Abengalvón,
"quanta riquiza tiene aver la yemos nos.
"Tan en salvo lo abremos commo lo de Carrión;
"nunqua avrié derecho de nos el Çid Campeador."
Quando esta falssedad dizién los de Carrión,

"We commend you to God, Doña Elvira and Doña Sol;
behave in such a way as to give us pleasure."
His sons-in-law replied: "May it so please God!"
Great was the sorrow at the time of leavetaking.
Both father and daughters wept emotionally,
and so did the Champion's knights.
"Listen, nephew Félez Muñoz!
you will go by way of Molina de Aragón, where you will spend a night;
give my regards to my friend the Moor Ibn Ghalbun:
he is to give my sons-in-law the best possible welcome;
tell him I'm sending my daughters to the lands of Carrión;
he is to see to all their needs to their satisfaction
and then escort them as far as Medinaceli for my sake.
For whatever he does for them I shall reward him richly."
They separated like the fingernail from the flesh.
Now the man born in a lucky hour returned to Valencia.
The young lords of Carrión began their journey;
they made a stop at Albarracín,
then the young lords of Carrión hastened on at top speed;
now they were in Molina with the Moor Ibn Ghalbun.
When the Moor heard of their arrival, he was heartily pleased;
he rode out to meet them with great delight;
how well he saw to their every want!
The following morning he rode out with them,
ordering an escort of two hundred horsemen for them;
they crossed the forests called the forests of Luzón,
they crossed the plain of Arbujuelo and reached the Jalón river,
stopping at the place called El Ansarera.[29]
The Moor gave his gifts to the Cid's daughters,
and a good horse apiece to the young lords of Carrión;
the Moor did all this out of love for the Cid and Champion.
Seeing the wealth that the Moor brought forth,
the two brothers plotted a treacherous act:
"Since we're going to abandon the Cid's daughters,
if we could kill the Moor Ibn Ghalbun
we would have all the riches he possesses.
It would be just as firmly ours as what we have in Carrión;
the Cid and Champion would never gain redress from us."
When those of Carrión uttered those disloyal words,

---

29. Not firmly identified.

un moro latinado bien gelo entendió;
non tiene poridad, díxolo Âbengalvón:
"Acáyaz, cúriate destos, ca eres mio señor:
"tu muert odí conssejar a ifantes de Carrión."
127. El moro Abengalvón, mucho era buen barragán,
con dozientos que tiene iva cavalgar;
armas iva teniendo, parós ante los ifantes;
de lo que el moro dixo a los ifantes non plaze:
"Si no lo dexás por mio Çid el de Bivar,
"tal cosa vos faría que por el mundo sonás,
"e luego levaría sus fijas al Campeador leal;
"vos nunqua en Carrión entrariedes jamás.
128. "¡Dezidme, qué vos fiz, ifantes de Carrión!
"yo sirviéndovos sin art, e vos conssejastes mie muort.
"Aquim parto de vos commo de malos e de traydores.
"Iré con vuestra graçia, don Elvira e doña Sol;
"poco preçio las nuevas de los de Carrión.
"Dios lo quiera e lo mande, que de tod el mundo es señor,
"d' aqueste casamiento ques grade el Campeador."
Esto les ha dicho, e el moro se tornó;
teniendo iva armas al troçir de Salón;
quommo de buen seso a Molina se tornó.
Ya movieron del Anssarera ifantes de Carrión,
acójense a andar de día e de noch;
a ssiniestro dexan Atiença, una peña muy fuort,
la sierra de Miedes passáronla estoz,
por los Montes Claros aguijan a espolón;
assiniestro dexan a Griza que Álamos pobló,
allí son caños do a Elpha ençerró;
a diestro dexan a Sant Estevan, mas cade aluon.
Entrados son los ifantes al robredo de Corpes,
los montes son altos, las ramas pujan con las nuoves,
elas bestias fieras que andan aderredor.
Fallaron un vergel con una linpia fuont;
mandan fincar la tienda ifantes de Carrión,
con quantos que ellos traen i yazen essa noch,
con sus mugieres en braços demuéstranles amor;
¡mal gelo cunplieron quando salié el sol!

they were clearly understood by a Moor who knew Spanish;
he didn't keep it secret, but told it to Ibn Ghalbun:
"Governor, watch out for these men, for you are my master:
I heard the young lords of Carrión plotting your death."
127. The Moor Ibn Ghalbun was a hardy fellow;
he rode out with his two hundred men;
putting on a military display, he appeared before the young lords;
the young lords were displeased by what the Moor said:
"If I weren't restrained by respect for My Cid, the lord of Vivar,
I would do something to you that would become known around the world,
and then I'd bring back the loyal Champion's daughters to him;
you would never get back to Carrión.
128. Tell me, what have I done to you, young lords of Carrión?
I served you without guile and you planned my death.
I depart from you here as from wicked, treacherous men.
I shall go with your permission, Doña Elvira and Doña Sol;
I little esteem the reputation of those of Carrión.
May God, who is Lord of the whole world, desire and decree
that the Champion derive pleasure from this marriage!"
This he said to them, and the Moor turned back;
he held military exercises on crossing the Jalón;
like the prudent man he was, he returned to Molina.
Now the young lords of Carrión left El Ansarera,
beginning to travel day and night;
on their left hand they passed by Atienza, a strongly fortified crag,
then they crossed the Miedes mountain range,[30]
and rode swiftly through Montes Claros;
on their left they passed by Griza, which was first settled by Álamos
(the caves in which he imprisoned Elpha are there);
on their right they passed by San Esteban de Gormaz, which is more distant.
The young lords entered the oak woods of Corpes;
the trees were tall, their boughs reaching the clouds,
and wild animals roamed about.
They found a clearing with a limpid spring;
the young lords of Carrión had their tent pitched;
with all their followers they spent that night there,
holding their wives in their arms and making love to them.
How ill they repaid them for it when the sun rose!

---

30. The places Miedes, Montes Claros, Griza, and Corpes, as well as the legendary
people Álamos and Elpha, are not firmly identified.

Mandaron cargar las azémilas con averes *a nombre,*
cogida han la tienda do albergaron de noch,
adelant eran idos los de criazón:
assí lo mandaron ifantes de Carrión,
que non i fincás ninguno, mugier nin varón,
si non amas sus mugieres doña Elvira e doña Sol:
deportar se quieren con ellas a todo su sabor.
Todos eran idos, ellos quatro solos son,
tanto mal comidieron ifantes de Carrión:
"Bien lo creades, don Elvira e doña Sol,
"aquí seredes escarnidas en estos fieros montes.
"Oy nos partiremos, e dexadas seredes de nos;
"non abredes part en tierras de Carrión.
"Irán aquestos mandados al Çid Campeador;
"nos vengaremos aquesta por la del león."
Allí les tuellen los mantos e los pelliçones,
páranlas en cuerpos y en camisas y en çiclatones.
Espuelas tienen calçadas los malos traydores,
en mano prenden las çinchas fuertes e duradores.
Quando esto vieron las dueñas, fablava doña Sol:
"Por Dios vos rogamos, don Díago e don Ferrando;
"dos espadas tenedes fuertes e tajadores,
"al una dizen Colada e al otra Tizón,
"cortandos las cabeças, mártires seremos nos.
"Moros e cristianos departirán desta razón,
"que por lo que nos mereçemos no lo prendemos nos.
"Atan malos enssienplos non fagades sobre nos:
"si nos fuéremos majadas, abiltaredes a vos;
retraer vos lo an en vistas o en cortes."
Lo que ruegan las dueñas non les ha ningún pro.
Essora les conpieçan a dar ifantes de Carrión;
con las çinchas corredizas májanlas tan sin sabor,
con las espuelas agudas, don ellas an mal sabor,
ronpién las camisas e las carnes a ellas amas a dos:
linpia salié la sangre sobre los çiclatones.
Ya lo sienten ellas en los sos coraçones.
¡Quál ventura serié esta, si ploguiesse al Criador
que assomasse essora el Çid Campeador!
Tanto las majaron que sin cosimente son;
sangrientas en las camisas e todos los çiclatones.
Canssados son de ferir ellos amos a dos,

They ordered the pack animals loaded with numerous goods,
they struck the tent in which they had slept overnight,
and their retinue went on ahead,
in obedience to the orders of the young lords of Carrión:
no one was to remain there, woman or man,
except their two wives, Doña Elvira and Doña Sol,
for they wished to sport with them to their heart's content.
All the others had gone, only those four were there,
so evil were the thoughts of the young lords of Carrión:
"Take our word for it, Doña Elvira and Doña Sol,
here in this wild forest you are to be put to shame.
We two will depart today, and you will be abandoned by us;
you'll have no share in the lands of Carrión.
News of this will reach the Cid and Champion;
this will be our revenge for the incident with the lion."
Then they removed the women's mantles and pelisses,
leaving them in their underwear: shifts and brocade drawers.
The treacherous villains were wearing spurs,
and they seized strong, tough girths.
When the ladies saw this, Doña Sol said:
"For God's sake we beg you, Don Diego and Don Fernando:
you have two strong, sharp swords,
one called Colada and the other, Tizona;
cut off our heads and we will be martyrs.
Everyone, Moor and Christian, will censure this action
because we don't consider that we deserve it.
Don't treat us with such evil cruelty:
if we were beaten, you would be cheapening yourselves;
you'll be reproached for it at formal meetings or in parliaments."
The ladies' request did them no good.
The young lords of Carrión then began to beat them;
they bruised them grievously with the buckled girths
and cut them with their sharp spurs, causing them great anguish,
tearing their shifts and wounding both women's flesh:
their bright blood flowed onto their brocade garments.
They now felt the full mental pain of it.
How fortunate it would have been, had it pleased the Creator
to have the Cid and Champion appear at that moment!
They beat them so hard that welts sprang up;
their shifts and drawers were all bloody.
The two brothers grew tired of beating them

ensayandos amos quál dará mejores colpes.
Ya non pueden fablar don Elvira e doña Sol,
por muertas las dexaron en el robredo de Corpes.
129. Leváronles los mantos e las pieles armiñas,
mas déxanlas marridas en briales y en camisas,
e a las aves del monte e a las bestias de la fiera guisa.
Por muertas las dexaron, sabed, que non por bivas.
¡Quál ventura serié si assomás essora el Cid *Roy Díaz!*
130. Ifantes de Carrión por muertas las dexaron,
que el una al otra nol torna recabdo.
Por los montes do ivan, ellos ívanse alabando:
"De nuestros casamientos agora somos vengados.
"Non las deviemos tomar por varraganas, si non fossemos rogados,
"pues nuestras parejas non eran pora en braços.
"La desondra del león assís irá vengando."
131. Alabandos ivan ifantes de Carrión.
Mas yo vos diré d' aquel Félez Muñoz;
sobrino era del Çid Campeador;
mandáronle ir adelante, mas de so grado non fo.
En la carrera do iva doliól el coraçon,
de todos los otros aparte se salió,
en un monte espesso Félez Muñoz se metió,
fasta que viesse venir sus primas amas a dos
o que an fecho ifantes de Carrión.
Víolos venir e odió una razón,
ellos nol vidien ni dend sabién ración;
sabed bien que si ellos le vidiessen, non escapara de muort.
Vansse los ifantes, aguijan a espolón.
Por el rastro tornós Félez Muñoz,
falló sus primas amorteçidas amas a dos.
Llamando: "¡primas, primas!" luego descavalgó,
arrendó el cavallo, a elas adeliñó;
"Ya primas, las mis primas, don Elvira e doña Sol,
"¡mal se ensayaron ifantes de Carrión!
"¡A Dios plega que dent prendan ellos mal galardón!"
Valas tornando a ellas amas a dos;
tanto son de traspuestas que nada dezir non puoden.
Partiéronsele las telas de dentro del coraçón,
llamando: "¡Primas, primas, don Elvira e doña Sol!
"¡Despertedes, primas, por amor del Criador!
"mientra es el día, ante que entre la noch,

and trying to see who could hit harder.
Doña Elvira and Doña Sol were no longer able to speak;
they were left for dead in the oak woods of Corpes.
129. The brothers took away with them their wives' mantles and ermine furs,
leaving them unconscious in their drawers and shifts,
at the mercy of the forest birds and ferocious animals.
I'll have you know, they left them for dead, unaware they were still alive.
How fortunate it would have been had the Cid Ruy.Díaz turned up just then!
130. The young lords of Carrión left them for dead,
neither woman being able to help the other.
As they rode through the forest, they boasted:
"Now we've avenged ourselves for our marriages.
We shouldn't have taken them even as concubines, if not urged to do so,
since they weren't a match for us as legitimate wives.
In this way that insult connected with the lion will be avenged."
131. The young lords of Carrión continued to swagger.
But now I shall tell you about that Félez Muñoz,
who was the nephew of the Cid and Champion;
he had been ordered to move ahead, but he did so unwillingly.
On his path his heart misgave him;
he separated himself from all the rest,
and entered a dense patch of woods,
waiting for his two cousins to come
or trying to see what the young lords of Carrión had done.
He saw the brothers coming and heard their conversation;
they didn't see him and were unaware of his presence;
you may be sure that, had they seen him, he wouldn't have escaped alive.
The young lords moved past, spurring their horses.
Félez Muñoz returned by that trail
and found his two cousins unconscious.
Shouting "Cousins, cousins!," he dismounted at once,
tied his horse's reins to a tree, and went over to the ladies;
"O cousins, my cousins, Doña Elvira and Doña Sol,
the young lords of Carrión have exerted themselves in an evil fashion!
May it please God that they be evilly repaid for it!"
He tried to restore them both to consciousness;
they were in such a deep swoon that they couldn't speak.
His heart was breaking.
He shouted: "Cousins, cousins, Doña Elvira and Doña Sol!
Wake up, cousins, for the Creator's sake,
while there's still daylight, before night falls,

"¡los ganados fieros non nos coman en aqueste mont!"
Van recordando don Elvira e doña Sol,
abrieron los ojos e vieron a Félez Muñoz.
"¡Esforçadvos, primas, por amor del Criador!
"De que non me fallaren ifantes de Carrión,
"a grant priessa seré buscado yo;
"si Dios non nos vale, aquí morremos nos."
Tan a grant duelo fablava doña Sol:
"sí vos lo meresca, mio primo, nuestro padre el Canpeador,
"dandos del agua, sí vos vala el Criador."
Con un sombrero que tiene Félez Muños,
nuevo era e fresco, que de Valençial sacó,
cogió del agua en el*le* e a sus primas dió;
mucho son lazradas e amas las fartó.
Tanto las rogó fata que las assentó.
Valas conortando e metiendo coraçón
fata que esfuerçan, e amas las tomó
e privado en el cavallo las cavalgó;
con el so manto a amas las cubrió,
el cavallo priso por la rienda e luego dent las part*ió*.
Todos tres señeros por los robredos de Corpes,
entre noch e día salieron de los montes;
a las aguas de Duero ellos arribados son,
a la torre de don Urraca elle las dexó.
A Sant Estevan vino Félez Muñoz,
falló a Dí*a*g Téllez el que de Álbar Fáñez f*o;*
quando elle lo o*di*ó, pesól de coraçón;
priso bestias e vestidos de pro,
hiva reçebir a don Elvira e a doña Sol;
en Sant Estevan dentro las metió,
quanto él mejor puede allí las ondró.
Los de Sant Estevan, siempre mesurados son,
quando sabién esto, pesóles de coraçón;
a llas fijas del Çid danles en*ff*urçi*ón.*
Allí sovieron ellas fata que sanas son.
Alabándos se*dí*an ifantes de Carrión.
Por todas essas tierras estas nuevas sabidas son;
de cuer pesó esto al buen rey don Alfons.
Van aquestos mandados a Valençia la mayor;
quando gelo dizen a mio Çid el Campeador,
una grand ora penssó e comidió;

so the wild beasts don't eat us in this forest!"
Doña Elvira and Doña Sol slowly came to their senses,
opened their eyes, and beheld Félez Muñoz.
"Make an effort, cousins, for the Creator's sake!
As soon as the young lords of Carrión find me missing,
I will be sought for urgently;
if God doesn't protect us, we shall die here."
Doña Sol said in great distress:
"May our father, the Champion, repay you for this, cousin;
give us some water, so may the Creator keep you!"
Félez Muñoz, with the hat he was wearing,
a brand new one he had brought along from Valencia,
scooped up some water and gave it to his cousins;
they were in very bad shape, and it soothed them both.
He kept on begging them to sit up until they did.
He comforted them and instilled courage in them
until they made an effort and he took them both
and quickly seated them on his horse;
he covered both of them with his cape,
took the horse by the reins, and led them away at once.
The three of them traversed the Corpes oak woods alone,
emerging from the forest at twilight;
they reached the river Duero
and he left them at La Torre ["the tower of Princess Urraca"].
Félez Muñoz came to San Esteban de Gormaz,
where he found Diego Téllez, formerly one of Álvar Fáñez's men;
when he heard what had occurred, he was deeply grieved;
he took mounts and good clothing
and went to pick up Doña Elvira and Doña Sol;
he lodged them in San Esteban,
doing them all the honor he could there.
When the people of San Esteban, who are always kindly,
learned about it, they were deeply grieved;
they offered the Cid's daughters hospitality befitting their station.
There they remained until they were well.
The young lords of Carrión continued to swagger.
The news was learned throughout the region;
it heartily grieved good King Alfonso.
The report reached mighty Valencia;
when it was told to My Cid the Champion,
he reflected and meditated for a long while;

alçó la su mano, a la barba se tomó:
"¡Grado a Cristus, que del mundo es señor,
"quando tal ondra me an dada ifantes de Carrión;
"par aquesta barba que nadi non messó,
"non la lograrán ifantes de Carrión;
"que a mis fijas bien las casaré yo!"
Pesó a mio Çid e a toda su cort,
e Álbar Fáñez d' alma e de coraçón.
Cavalgó Minaya con Per Vermu*doz*
e Martín Antolínez, el Burgalés de pro,
con dozientos cavalleros, quales mio Çid mandó;
dixoles fuertemientre que andidiessen de día e de noch,
aduxiessen a ssus fijas a Valençia la mayor.
Non lo detardan el mandado de *so* señor,
apriessa cavalgan, andan los días e las noches;
vinieron a Gormaz, un castiello tan fu*o*rt,
hi albergaron por verdad una noch.
A Sant Estevan el mandado llegó
que vinié Minaya por sus primas amas a dos.
Varones de Sant Estevan, a guisa de muy pro*es*,
reçiben a Minaya e a todos *sos* varones,
presentan a Minaya essa noch grant enffurçión;
non gelo quiso tomar, mas mucho gelo gradió:
"Graçias, varones de Sant Estevan, que sodes coñosçedores,
"por aquesta ondra que vos diestes a esto que nos cuntió;
"mucho vos lo gradeçe, allá do está, mio Çid el Canpeador;
"assí lo ffago yo que aquí estó.
"¡Affé Dios de los çielos que vos dé dent buen galardón!"
Todos gelo gradeçen e sos pagados son,
adeliñan a posar pora folgar essa noch.
Minaya va ve*er* su*es* primas do son,
en el*le* fincan los ojos don Elvira e doña Sol:
"Atanto vos lo gradimos commo si viéssemos al Criador;
"e vos a él lo gradid, quando bivas somos nos.
"En los días de vagar, *en Valençia la mayor,*
"toda nuestra rencura sabremos contar *nos.*"

he raised his hand and clutched his beard;
"I thank Christ, who is Lord of the world,
since the young lords of Carrión have done me such honor;
by this beard, which no one has ever plucked,
the young lords of Carrión won't get away with it;
I shall find good husbands for my daughters!"
My Cid and all his followers were deeply grieved,
as was Álvar Fáñez in his heart and soul.
Minaya rode out with Pedro Bermúdez
and Martín Antolínez, that excellent man from Burgos,
and the two hundred horsemen My Cid had assigned;
he had given them strict orders to ride by day and night
and bring home his daughters to mighty Valencia.
They didn't hesitate to carry out their lord's command;
they rode swiftly both by day and by night,
arriving at Gormaz, a strong castle,
where they did indeed spend one night.
The news reached San Esteban
that Minaya was coming for his two cousins.
The men of San Esteban, as the fine folk they were,
welcomed Minaya and all his men,
offering Minaya great hospitality that night;
he didn't want to accept it, but thanked them for it effusively:
"Thank you, men of San Esteban, you that are so kindly,
for the honor you have done to us on this occasion;
My Cid the Champion, back in Valencia, is very grateful to you,
just as I am, right here.
May God in heaven give you a good reward for it!"
They all thanked him, feeling pleased,
and they headed for their lodgings to relax that night.
Minaya went to see his cousins where they were housed;
Doña Elvira and Doña Sol gazed at him fixedly:
"We thank you as much as if we were seeing the Creator;
thank him and yourself for finding us alive.
In days of greater leisure, in mighty Valencia,
we'll be able to recount all our bitterness."

[SUMMARY of strophes **132–134** (verses 2863–2984): The Cid's lieu-
tenants, promising vengeance, take his daughters back to Valencia.
The Cid sends Muño Gustioz to King Alfonso requesting a formal as-
sembly to judge the affair; Gustioz finds the king in Sahagún. Alfonso,

[**Tiradas 135–146** (versos 2985–3371):]
135. Ya les va pesando a ifantes de Carrión,
por que en Toledo el rey fazié cort;
miedo han que i verná mio Çid el Campeador.
Prenden so conssejo, assí parientes commo son,
ruegan al rey que los quite desta cort.
Dixo el rey: No lo feré, ¡sín salve Dios!
"ca i verná mio Çid el Campeador;
"darlêdes derecho, ca rencura ha de vos.
"Qui lo fer non quisiesse, o no ir a mi cort,
"quite mio reyno, ca dél non he sabor."
Ya lo vidieron que es a fer ifantes de Carrión,
prenden conssejo parientes commo son;
el comde don Garçía en estas nuevas fo,
enemigo de mio Çid, que mal siemprel buscó,
aqueste conssejó los ifantes de Carrión.
Llegava el plazdo, querién ir a la cort;
en los primeros va el buen rey don Alfons,
el comde don Anrric y el comde don Remond,
—aqueste fo padre del buen enperador,—
el comde don Fróila y el comde don Birbón.
Foron i de so reyno otros muchos sabidores,
de toda Castiella todos los mejores.
El comde don Garçía, *el Crespo de Grañón,*
e Álvar Díaz el que Oca mandó,
e Ansuor Gonçálvez *e* Gonçalvo Ansuórez,
e Per Ansuórez, sabet, allís açertó,
e Díago e Ferrando i son amos a dos,
e con ellos grand bando que aduxieron a la cort:
enbaír le cuydan a mio Çid el Campeador.
De todas partes allí juntados son.
Aun non era llegado el que en buen ora naçió,
por que se tarda el rey non ha sabor.

acknowledging his responsibility for the disastrous double marriage, convokes a major assembly, to meet in Toledo in seven weeks. Gustioz returns to Valencia.]

[**Strophes 135–146** (verses 2985–3371):]

135. Now the young lords of Carrión were grieved
because the king was holding a general assembly in Toledo.
They were afraid that My Cid the Champion would come there.
They and all their relatives conferred together
and asked the king to exempt them from attending.
The king said: "No, I won't, so may God save me!
For My Cid the Champion will be there;
you shall make amends to him, for he has a grievance against you.
Whoever refuses, and fails to attend my assembly,
is to leave my kingdom, because I don't want him here."
Now the young lords of Carrión saw that they had to comply;
they and all their relatives conferred;
Count García participated,
that enemy of My Cid, ever seeking to harm him;
he too gave advice to the young lords of Carrión.
The appointed day arrived, all were about to assemble;
among the foremost were good King Alfonso,
Count Enrique and Count Raimundo
(the latter was the father of the good emperor[31])
Count Froila and Count Birbón.[32]
From his kingdom many other legal experts attended,
all the best in Castile.
Count García, "the curlyhead from Grañón,"
and Álvar Díaz, who governed Oca,
and Ansur González and Gonzalo Ansúrez
and Pedro Ansúrez, I'll have you know, were also there,[33]
as well as both Diego and Fernando,
and with them a large faction which they brought to the assembly,
intending to thwart My Cid the Champion.
They gathered there from all parts.
The man born in a lucky hour had not yet arrived,
and the king was displeased at his delay.

---

31. Raimundo, governor of Galicia, was the father of Alfonso VII; Enrique was related to the dukes of Burgundy; Froila was count of León.   32. Others read "Beltrán."
33. The last three were elder brother, father, and uncle, respectively, of the young lords of Carrión.

Al quinto día venido es mio Çid el Campeador;
Âlvar Fáñez adelantel enbió,
que besasse las manos al rey so señor:
bien lo sopiesse que i serié essa noch.
Quando lo odió el rey, plógol de coraçón;
con grandes yentes el rey cavalgó
e iva reçebir al que en buen ora naçió.
Bien aguisado viene el Çid con todos los sos,
buenas conpañas que assí an tal señor.
Quando lo ovo a ojo el buen rey don Alfons,
firiós a tierra mio Çid el Campeador;
biltar se quiere e ondrar a so señor.
Quando lo *vido* el rey, por nada non tardó;
"¡Par sant Esidre, verdad non será oy!
"Cavalgad, Çid; si non, non avría dend sabor;
"saludar nos hemos d' alma e de coraçón.
"De lo que a vos pesa a mí duele el coraçón;
"¡Dios lo mande que por vos se ondre oy la cort!"
"—Amen", dixo mio Çid, el *buen* Campeador;
besóle la mano e después le saludó;
"Grado a Dios, quando vos veo, señor.
"Omíllom a vos e al comde do Remond
"e al comde don Arric e a quantos que i son;
"¡Dios salve a nuestros amigos e a vos más, señor!
"Mi mugier doña Ximena, —dueña es de pro,—
"bésavos las manos, e mis fijas amas a dos,
"desto que nos abino que vos pese, señor."
Respondió el rey: "¡sí fago, sín salve Dios!"
136. Pora Toledo el rey tornada da;
essa noch mio Çid Tajo non quiso passar:
"¡Merçed, ya rey, sí el Criador vos salve!
"Penssad, señor, de entrar a la cibdad,
"e yo con los mios posaré a San Serván:
"las mis compañas esta noche llegarán.
"Terné vigilia en aqueste santo logar;
"cras mañana entraré a la çibdad,
"e iré a la cort enantes de yantar."
Dixo el rey: "plazme de veluntad."
El rey don Alfons a Toledo *va* entrar;

On the fifth day My Cid the Champion came;
he sent ahead Álvar Fáñez
to kiss the hands of his lord the king
and let him know he'd be there that night.
When the king heard this, he was glad at heart;
the king rode out with many followers
to greet the man born in a lucky hour.
The Cid and all his men were well equipped,
good troops as befitted a master such as he.
When good King Alfonso caught sight of him,
My Cid the Champion dismounted
and began to prostrate himself in honor of his lord.
When the king saw that, he hastened to say:
"By Saint Isidore, this shall not be!
Mount your steed, Cid, or else I'll be displeased;
we must embrace with heart and soul.
Whatever grieves you pains my heart;
may God grant that the assembly is honored by you today!"
"Amen," said My Cid, the good Champion;
he kissed the king's hand and then embraced him;
"I thank God when I see you, sire.
I humble myself before you and Count Raimundo
and Count Enrique and all the rest;
may God save our friends and especially you, sire!
My wife Doña Jimena, an excellent lady,
kisses your hands, and so do my two daughters,
hoping you are grieved at what has befallen us, sire."
The king replied: "I *am*, so may God save me!"
136. The king returned to Toledo;
that night My Cid refused to cross the Tajo:
"Grace, O king, so may the Creator save you!
Sire, go on and enter the city,
while I and my men lodge in San Servando:[34]
my troops will arrive tonight.
I shall keep vigil in that holy place;
early tomorrow morning I shall enter the city,
and I shall be at the assembly before eating a meal."
The king said: "That's all right with me."
King Alfonso returned to Toledo,

---

34. A monastery just outside the city.

mio Çid Roy Díaz en Sant Serván posar.
Mandó fazer candelas e poner en el altar;
sabor a de velar en essa santidad,
al Criador rogando e fablando en poridad.
Entre Minaya e los buenos que i ha
acordados foron, quando vino la man.
137. Matines e prima dixieron faza los albores,
suelta fo la missa antes que saliesse el sol,
e ssu ofrenda han fecha muy buena e *a sazón.*
"Vos, Minaya Álbar Fáñez, el mio braço mejor,
"vos iredes conmigo e obispo don Jerome
"e Per Vermudoz e aqueste Muño Gustioz
"e Martín Antolínez, el Burgalés de pro,
"e Álbar Albaroz e Álbar Salvadórez
"e Martín Muñoz, que en buen punto naçió,
"e mio sobrino Félez Muñoz;
"comigo irá Mal Anda, que es bien sabidor,
"e Galind Garçiez, el bueno d' Aragón;
"con estos cúnplansse çiento de los buenos que i son.
"Velmezes vestidos por sufrir las guarnizones,
"de suso las lorigas tan blancas commo el sol;
"sobre las lorigas armiños e pelliçones,
"e que no parescan las armas, bien presos los cordones;
"so los mantos las espadas dulçes e tajadores;
"d' aquesta guisa quiero ir a la cort,
"por demandar mios derechos e dezir mie razón.
"Si desobra buscaren ifantes de Carrión,
"do tales çiento tovier, bien seré sin pavor."
Respondieron todos: "nos esso queremos, señor."
Assí commo lo ha dicho, todos adobados son.
Nos detiene por nada el que en buen ora naçió:
calças de buen paño en sus camas metió,
sobrellas unos çapatos que a granta huebra son.
Vistió camisa de rançal tan blanca commo el sol,
con oro e con plata todas las presas son,
al puño bien están, ca él se lo mandó;
sobrella un brial primo de çiclatón,
obrado es con oro, pareçen por o son.
Sobresto una piel vermeja, las bandas d' oro son,
siempre la viste mio Çid el Campeador.
Una cofia sobre los pelos d' un escarín de pro,

My Cid Ruy Díaz lodged in San Servando.
He ordered tapers lit and placed on the altar;
he felt like keeping vigil in that holy atmosphere,
praying to the Creator and formulating secret plans.
Minaya and the other good men there
had come to an agreement by morning.
137. Matins and prime were sung a little before dawn,
and mass was over before the sun rose;
they made their offering, which was very good and proper.
"You, Minaya Álvar Fáñez, my right hand,
will go with me and Bishop Jérôme
and Pedro Bermúdez and Muño Gustioz
and Martín Antolínez, that excellent man from Burgos,
and Álvar Álvarez and Álvar Salvadórez
and Martín Muñoz, who was born at a propitious moment,
and my nephew Félez Muñoz;
with me will be Mal Anda, who is learned in law,
and Galín García, that good man from Aragon;
they will be among the hundred of my good men here.
Put on inner tunics to avoid chafing from your armor;
over them, coats of mail shining like the sun;
over the mail, ermines and pelisses,
with strings drawn tightly so the armor doesn't show;
beneath your capes, well-tempered, sharp swords;
in that fashion I wish to attend the assembly
to claim my rights and state my case.
If the young lords of Carrión should make some insidious trouble,
I won't be afraid of even a hundred such as they."
They all replied: "As you wish, my lord."
They all dressed according to his orders.
The man born in a lucky hour now made no delay:
he clad his legs in good woolen hose;
over them, he put on shoes richly adorned.
He wore a linen shirt that shone like the sun,
all its fastenings adorned with gold and silver;
they were snug at the wrists, for he had ordered it so;
over the shirt, a superb outer tunic of silk brocade,
worked with gold; his garments gleamed wherever they were seen.
On top of that, the red fur coat with golden belts
which My Cid the Champion always wore.
On his hair, a cap of excellent linen,

con oro es obrada, fecha por razón,
que nol contalassen los pelos al buen Çid Campeador;
la barba avié luenga e prísola con el cordón,
por tal lo faze esto que recabdar quiere todo lo *so*.
De suso cubrió un manto que es de grant valor,
en el*le* abrién que ve*er* quantos que i son.
Con aquestos çiento que adobar mandó,
apriessa cavalga, de San Serván salió;
assí iva mio Çid adobado a lla cort.
A la puerta de fuera descavalga a sabor;
cuerdamientre entra mio Çid con todos los sos:
el*le* va en medio, elos çiento aderredor.
Quando lo vieron entrar al que en buen ora naçió
levantós en pie el buen rey don Alfons
e el co*m*de don Anrric e el co*m*de don Remont
e desí adelant, sabet, todos los otros *de la cort:*
a grant ondra lo reçiben al que en buen ora naçió.
Nos quiso levantar el Crespo de Grañón,
nin todos los del bando de ifantes de Carrión.
El rey a *mio* Çid *a las manos le tomó:*
"Venid acá s*eer comigo,* Campeador,
"en aqueste escaño quem diestes vos en don;
"maguer que âlgunos pesa, mejor sodes que nos."
Essora dixo muchas merçedes el que Valençia gañó:
"se*ed* en vuestro escaño commo rey e señor;
"acá posaré con todos aquestos mios."
Lo que dixo el Çid al rey plogo de coraçón.
En un escaño torniño essora mio Çid posó,
los çiento quel aguardan posan aderredor.
Catando están a mio Çid quantos ha en la cort,
a la barba que avié luenga e presa con el cordón;
en sos aguisamientos bien semeja varón.
Nol pueden catar de vergüença ifantes de Carrión.
Essora se levó en pie el buen rey don Alfons;
"¡Oíd, mesnadas, sí vos vala el Criador!
"Yo, de que fu rey, non fiz más de dos cortes:
"la una f*o* en Burgos, e la otra en Carrión,
"esta terçera a Toledo la vin fer oy,
"por el amor de mio Çid el que en buen ora naçió,

worked with gold, made to order,
so that no one could pull out the hair of the good Cid and Champion;
his beard was long and caught up by a string;
this was so that his entire person would be protected.
Over all that, he wore a very expensive cape,
which everyone present would be compelled to admire.
With those hundred men whom he had ordered equipped
he rode out urgently, leaving San Servando;
thus attired, My Cid proceeded to the assembly.
Outside the door he dismounted gracefully;
My Cid and all his men entered quietly,
he in the middle, the other hundred around him.
When the man born in a lucky hour was seen entering,
good King Alfonso stood up,
as did Count Enrique and Count Raimundo
and one by one, I'll have you know, everyone else in the assembly:
they welcomed with great honor the man born in a lucky hour.
The curlyheaded man from Grañón refused to rise,
as did the entire faction of the young lords of Carrión.
The king took My Cid by the hands:
"Come sit here with me, Champion,
on this bench which you gave me as a gift;[35]
even if it grieves some people, you are better than we are."
Then the conqueror of Valencia uttered many thanks:
"Sit on your bench, as our king and lord;
I shall sit there with all those followers of mine."
What the Cid said pleased the king heartily.
Then My Cid sat down on a bench of turned wood;
the hundred men guarding him sat all around him.
My Cid was observed by everyone in the assembly,
as was his long beard caught up with a string;
his attire made him look quite virile.
The young lords of Carrión couldn't look at him, out of shame.
Then good King Alfonso arose:
"Hear me, my subjects, so may the Creator keep you!
Ever since I have been king, I have called only two general assemblies;
one was in Burgos, the other in Carrión;
I've summoned this third one in Toledo today
for the sake of My Cid, the man born in a lucky hour,

---

35. This was never narrated.

"que reçiba derecho de ifantes de Carrión.
"Grande tuerto le han tenido, sabémoslo todos nos;
"alcaldes sean desto comde don Anrric e comde don Remond
"e estos otros comdes que del vando non sodes.
"Todos meted i mientes, ca sodes coñoscedores,
"por escoger el derecho, ca tuerto non mando yo.
"Della e della part en paz seamos oy.
"Juro par sant Esidre, el que bolviere mi cort
"quitar me a el reyno, perderá mi amor.
"Con el que toviere derecho yo dessa parte me so.
"Agora demande mio Çid el Campeador:
"sabremos qué responden ifantes de Carrión."
Mio Çid la mano besó al rey e en pie se levantó;
"Mucho vos lo gradesco commo a rey e a señor,
"por quanto esta cort fiziestes por mi amor.
"Esto les demando a ifantes de Carrión:
"por mis fijas quem dexaron yo non he desonor,
"ca vos las casastes, rey, sabredes qué fer oy;
"mas quando sacaron mis fijas de Valençia la mayor,
"yo bien los quería d' alma e de coraçón,
"diles dos espadas a Colada e a Tizón
"—estas yo las gané a guisa de varón,—
"ques ondrassen con ellas e sirviessen a vos;
"quando dexaron mis fijas en el robredo de Corpes,
"comigo non quisieron aver nada e perdieron mi amor;
"denme mis espadas quando mios yernos no son."
Atorgan los alcaldes: "tod esto es razón."
Dixo comde don García: "a esto fablemos nos."
Essora salién aparte ifantes de Carrión,
con todos sos parientes y el bando que i son;
apriessa lo ivan trayendo e acuerdan la razón:
"Aun grand amor nos faze el Çid Campeador,
"quando desondra de sus fijas no nos demanda oy;
"bien nos abendremos con el rey don Alfons.
"Démosle sus espadas, quando assí finca la boz,
"e quando las toviere, partir se a la cort;
"ya mas non avrá derecho de nos el Çid Canpeador."
Con aquesta fabla tornaron a la cort;
"¡Merçed, ya rey don Alfons, sodes nuestro señor!
"No lo podemos negar, ca dos espadas nos dio;
"quando las demanda e dellas ha sabor,

so he can obtain redress from the young lords of Carrión.
He has been grievously wronged, as we all know;
judges in the case will be Count Enrique and Count Raimundo
and you other counts who don't belong to any faction.
All of you are to apply yourselves (for you are legal experts)
to see justice done, for I give no unjust orders.
On both sides let us be in peace today.
I swear by Saint Isidore: anyone causing a row in my assembly
must leave my kingdom and lose my favor.
I will side with whichever party is judged to be in the right.
Now let My Cid the Champion proffer his complaint;
then we'll hear what the young lords of Carrión have to say in reply."
My Cid kissed the king's hand and arose:
"I am very grateful to you as my king and lord
for convening this assembly on my account.
With this I charge the young lords of Carrión:
Their abandonment of my daughters does not dishonor me,
because *you* gave them away, sire, and you'll know how to act today;
but when they took my daughters from mighty Valencia
I loved these young men with heart and soul
and gave them the two swords Colada and Tizona,
which I had won manfully,
for them to use gaining honor for themselves and serving you;
when they deserted my daughters in the oak woods at Corpes,
they broke off relations with me and lost my favor;
let them return my swords, since they are no longer my sons-in-law."
The judges agreed: "All this is just."
Count García said: "Allow us to discuss it."
Then the young lords of Carrión went out to a private place
with all their relatives and the faction they had there;
they quickly deliberated and agreed to the request:
"The Cid and Champion is actually treating us very leniently
by not charging us today with dishonoring his daughters;
we'll come to an amicable settlement with King Alfonso.
Let's give back his swords, if that's the sum total of his claim,
and when he gets them the assembly will be dismissed;
the Cid and Champion will have no further complaint against us."
After that discussion they returned to the assembly:
"Grace, O King Alfonso, you that are our lord!
We cannot deny that he gave us two swords;
if he claims them and wants them back,

"dárgelas queremos delant estando vos."
Sacaron las espadas Colada e Tizón,
pusiéronlas en mano del rey so señor;
sacan las espadas e relumbra toda la cort,
las maçanas e los arriazes todos d' oro son;
maravíllanse dellas los omnes buenos de la cort.
A mio Çid llamó el rey, las espadas le dio;
reçibió las espadas, las manos le besó,
tornos al escaño dont se levantó.
En las manos las tiene e amas las cató;
nos las pueden camear, ca el Çid bien las connosçe;
alegrósle tod el cuerpo, sonrrisós de coraçón,
alçava la mano, a la barba se tomó;
"par aquesta barba que nadi non messó,
"assís irán vengando don Elvira e doña Sol."
A so sobrino don Pero por nómbrel llamó,
tendió el braço, la espada Tizón le dio;
"Prendetla, sobrino, ca mejora en señor."
A Martín Antolínez, el Burgalés de pro,
tendió el braço, el espada Coládal dio;
"Martín Antolínez, mio vassallo de pro,
"prended a Colada, ganéla de buen señor,
"de Remont Verenguel de Barçilona la mayor.
"Por esso vos la do que la bien curiedes vos.
"Sé que si vos acaeçiere o viniere sazón,
"con ella ganaredes grand prez e grand valor."
Besóle la mano, el espada reçibió.
Luego se levantó mio Çid el Campeador;
"¡Grado al Criador e a vos, rey señor!
"ya pagado so de mis espadas, de Colada e de Tizón.
Otra rencura he de ifantes de Carrión:
"quando sacaron de Valencia mis fijas amas a dos,
"en oro e en plata tres mill marcos les dîo;
"yo faziendo esto, ellos acabaron lo so;
"denme mios averes, quando mios yernos non son."
¡Aquí veriedes quexarse ifantes de Carrión!
Dize el comde don Remond: "dezid de ssí o de no."
Essora responden ifantes de Carrión:
"Por essol diemos sus espadas al Çid Campeador,
"que al no nos demandasse, que aquí fincó la boz."
Allí les respondió el comde do Remond:

we are willing to return them to him in your presence."
They brought forth the swords Colada and Tizona
and placed them in the hands of the king their lord;
when the swords were drawn, the whole assembly was illuminated;
the pommels and quillons were all of gold;
the noblemen in the assembly were amazed at those swords.
The king called My Cid and handed him the swords;
he took them and kissed his hands,
then returned to the bench from which he had arisen.
He held them in his hands and scrutinized them both;
there was no way fakes could be substituted, for the Cid was very familiar with them;
he was extremely happy and gave a warm smile;
he raised his hand and clutched his beard:
"By this beard, which no one has ever plucked,
in this way Doña Elvira and Doña Sol will be avenged."
He called his nephew Don Pedro by name,
stretched out his arm, and gave him the sword Tizona:
"Take it, nephew; now it has a better owner."
To Martín Antolínez, the excellent man from Burgos,
he stretched out his arm and gave him the sword Colada:
"Martín Antolínez, my excellent vassal,
take Colada, which I won from a worthy owner,
Berenguer Ramón of mighty Barcelona.
I give it to you to take good care of it.
I know that if the occasion arises,
you will win fame for great bravery with it."
He kissed his hand and accepted the sword.
Then My Cid the Champion arose:
"I thank the Creator and you, sire!
I am satisfied as regards my swords Colada and Tizona.
But I have another charge against the young lords of Carrión:
When they took my two daughters from Valencia,
I gave them three thousand marks of gold and silver;
though I acted thus, they went and did their misdeed;
let them return my gift, since they are no longer my sons-in-law."
How the young lords of Carrión then complained!
Count Raimundo said: "Say yes or no."
Then the young lords of Carrión replied:
"We just gave our swords to the Cid Champion
so he'd make no further claims and the charges would end there."
Then Count Raimundo answered them:

"Si ploguiere al rey, assí dezimos nos:
"a lo que demanda el Çid quel recudades vos."
Dixo el buen rey: "assí lo otorgo yo."
Levantós en pie el Çid Campeador;
"Destos averes que vos di yo,
"si me los dades, o dedes dello razón."
Essora salién aparte ifantes de Carrión;
non acuerdan en conssejo, ca los averes grandes son:
espesos los han ifantes de Carrión.
Tornan con el conssejo e fablavan a sso sabor:
"Mucho nos afinca el que Valençia gañó;
"quando de nuestros averes assíl prende sabor,
"pagar le hemos de heredades en tierras de Carrión."
Dixieron los alcaldes quando manfestados son:
"Si esso ploguiere al Çid, non gelo vedamos nos;
"mas en nuestro juvizio assí lo mandamos nos,
"que aquí lo enterguedes dentro en la cort."
A estas palabras fabló rey don Alfons:
"Nos bien la sabemos, aquesta razón,
"que derecho demanda el Çid Campeador.
"Destos tres mil marcos los dozientos tengo yo;
"entramos me los dieron ifantes de Carrión.
"Tornárgelos quiero, ca tan desfechos son,
"enterguen a mio Çid el que en buen ora nació;
"quando ellos los an a pechar, non gelos quiero yo."
Ferrand Gonçálvez odredes qué fabló:
"averes monedados non tenemos nos."
Luego respondió el conde don Remond:
"el oro e la plata espendiésteslo vos;
"por juvizio lo damos antel rey don Alfons:
páguenle en apreçiadura e préndalo el Campeador."
Ya vieron que es a fer ifantes de Carrión.
Veriedes aduzir tanto cavallo corredor,
tanta gruessa mula, tanto palafré de sazón,
tanta buena espada con toda guarnizón;
recibiólo mio Çid commo apreçiaron en la cort.
Sobre los dozientos marcos que tenía el rey Alfons
pagaron los ifantes al que en buen ora nació;
enpréstanles de lo ageno, que non les cumple lo so.
Mal escapan jogados, sabed, desta razón.
138. Estas apreçiaduras mio Çid presas las ha,

"If it please the king, we say
that you must respond to the Cid's claim."
The good king said: "I concur with that."
The Cid Champion arose:
"That gift which I made to you,
either return it or account for it."
Then the young lords of Carrión had another private talk;
they found no solution because the amount was so great:
the young lords of Carrión had spent the money.
They returned with their reply, and spoke as they thought best:
"The conqueror of Valencia is bearing down very hard on us;
if he is so eager for our property,
we'll pay him in estates on the lands of Carrión."
After their declaration the judges said:
"If that satisfies the Cid, we have no objection;
but our judgment and command
is that you hand over the money right here in the assembly."
Hearing this, King Alfonso spoke:
"We are in agreement with that decision,
because the Cid and Champion's claim is just.
Of that three thousand marks, two hundred is in my possession;
the two young lords of Carrión gave me that amount.
I'm ready to give it back, seeing they're in such need;
let them hand it over to My Cid, who was born in a lucky hour;
since they have to pay it, I don't want it from them."
Fernán González spoke (you shall hear what he said):
"We have no ready cash."
Then Count Raimundo replied:
"You have spent the gold and silver;
the decision we pronounce before King Alfonso is:
let the Champion accept payment in kind."
Now the young lords of Carrión saw that they had to comply.
There you might see many swift horses being brought,
many stout mules, many fine palfreys,
many good swords with all their appurtenances;
My Cid accepted them at the judges' valuation.
Along with the two hundred marks that had belonged to King Alfonso,
the young lords paid their full debt to the man born in a lucky hour;
they had to borrow from others, because their own funds were insufficient.
I'll have you know, they got off that charge badly and with mockery.
138. My Cid had received that payment in kind;

sos omnes las tienen e dellas penssarán.
Mas quando esto ovo acabado, penssaron luego d'al.
"¡Merçed, *ya* rey señor, por amor de caridad!
"La rencura mayor non se me puede olbidar.
"Oídme toda la cort e pésevos de mio mal;
"ifantes de Carrión, quem desondraron tan mal,
"a menos de riebtos no los puedo dexar."
139. "Dezid ¿qué vos mereçí, ifantes *de Carrión*,
"en juego o en vero o en alguna razón?
"aquí lo mejoraré a juvizio de la cort.
"¿A quém descubriestes las telas del coraçón?
"A la salida de Valençia mis fijas vos di yo,
"con muy grand ondra e averes a nombre;
"quando las non queriedes, ya canes traidores,
"¿por qué las sacávades de Valençia sus honores?
"¿A qué las firiestes a çinchas e a espolones?
"Solas las dexastes en el robredo de Corpes,
"a las bestias fieras e a las aves del mont.
"Por quanto les fiziestes menos valedes vos.
"Si non recudedes, véalo esta cort."
140. El comde don Garçía en pie se levantava;
"¡Merçed, ya rey, el mejor de toda España!
"Vezós mio Çid a llas cortes pregonadas;
"dexóla creçer e luenga trae la barba;
"los unos le han miedo e los otros espanta.
"Los de Carrión son de natura ta*n* *alta,*
"non gelas devién querer sus fijas por varraganas,
"¿o quien gelas diera por parejas o por veladas?
"Derecho fizieron porque las han dexadas.
"Quanto él dize non gelo preçiamos nada."
Essora el Campeador prísos a la barba;
"¡Grado a Dios que çielo e tierra manda!
"por esso es luenga que a deliçio f*o* criada.
"¿Qué avedes vos, comde, por retraer la mi barba?
"ca de quando nasco a deliçio f*o* criada;
"ca non me priso a ella fijo de mugier nada,
"nimbla messó fijo de moro nin de cristiana,
"commo yo a vos, comde, en el castiello de Cabra.
"Quando pris a Cabra, e a vos por la barba,
"non i ovo rapaz que non messó su pulgada;
"la que yo messé aun non es eguada,

his men took charge of it and would tend to it further.
But when that activity was over, a new matter was raised at once.
"Grace, O sire, for Christian charity's sake!
The weightiest charge I cannot forget.
All in the assembly, hear me and grieve at my misfortune;
the young lords of Carrión, who dishonored me so basely,
I cannot let go without challenging them.
139. Tell me, what did I do to you, young lords of Carrión,
in sport or seriously, or in any fashion?
Here, if the assembly so decides, I shall make it up to you.
Why did you lay bare my heartstrings?
When you left Valencia I gave you my daughters
with great honor and numerous gifts;
if you didn't want them, you treacherous dogs,
why did you take them away from Valencia, their estate?
Why did you beat them with girths and spurs?
You deserted them alone in the oak woods of Corpes,
leaving them to the wild animals and the forest birds.
In so treating them, you forfeited your honor.
If you don't reply, let the judges look to it."
140. Count García arose:
"Grace, O king, the best in all Spain!
My Cid is well accustomed to convoked assemblies;
he has let his beard grow and wears it long;
some fear him, others are in awe of him.
Those of Carrión are of so lofty a lineage,
they shouldn't have wanted his daughters even as concubines;
who would have given them to them as suitable matches and legitimate wives?
They did the right thing by abandoning them.
We don't care an iota for anything he says."
Then the Champion clutched his beard:
"I thank God, who rules heaven and earth!
My beard is long because it has been grown carefully.
What right have you, count, to find fault with my beard?
For, since it first started growing, it has been carefully tended to;
no living man has ever grasped it,
nor has any son of Moor or Christian woman ever plucked it,
as I plucked yours, count, in the castle of Cabra.
When I took Cabra, and you by the beard,
there wasn't a youngster who didn't pluck out his little part of it;
the spot I plucked still doesn't match the rest,

"ca yo la trayo aquí en mi bolsa alçada."
141. Ferrán Gonçálvez en pie se levantó,
a altas vozes odredes qué fabló:
"Dexássedesvos, Çid, de aquesta razón;
"de vuestros averes de todos pagados ssodes.
"Non creciés varaja entre nos e vos.
"De natura somos de comdes de Carrión:
"deviemos casar con fijas de reyes o de enperadores,
"ca non perteneçién fijas de ifançones.
"Por que las dexamos derecho fiziemos nos;
"más nos preçiamos, sabet, que menos no."
142. Mío Çid Roy Díaz a Per Vermudoz cata;
"¡Fabla, Pero Mudo, varón que tanto callas!
"Yo las he fijas, e tú primas cormanas;
"a mí lo dizen, a tí dan las orejadas.
"Si yo respondier, tú non entrarás en armas."
143. Per Vermudoz conpeçó de fablar;
detiénesle la lengua, non puede delibrar,
mas quando enpieça, sabed, nol da vagar:
"Dirévos, Çid, costunbres avedes tales,
"siempre en las cortes Pero Mudo me llamades.
"Bien lo sabedes que yo non puodo más;
"por lo que yo ovier a fer por mí non mancará.
"Mientes, Ferrando, de quanto dicho has;
"por el Campeador mucho valiestes más.
"Las tues mañas yo te las sabré contar:
"miémbrat quando lidiamos çerca Valençia la grand;
"pedist las feridas primeras al Canpeador leal,
"vist un moro, fústel ensayar;
"antes fuxiste que a él te allegasses.
"Si yo non uviás, el moro te jugara mal;
"passé por tí, con el moro me of de ajuntar,
"de los primeros colpes ofle de arrancar;
"did el cavallo, tóveldo en poridad:
"fasta este día no lo descubrí a nadi.
"Delant mio Çid e delante todos ovístete de alabar
"que mataras el moro e que fizieras barnax;
"croviérontelo todos, mas non saben la verdad.
"¡E eres fermoso, mas mal varragán!
"Lengua sin manos, ¿quomo osas fablar?
144. "Di, Ferrando, otorga esta razón:

for I have the hair tucked away here in my purse."

141. Fernán González arose,
and loudly said what you shall now hear:
"Cid, you ought to drop this charge;
all your possessions have been returned to you.
Let the quarrel between us not escalate!
We are of the lineage of the counts of Carrión:
we ought to marry daughters of kings or emperors,
for daughters of minor noblemen don't suit us.
If we deserted them, we did right;
I'll have you know, we think more of ourselves for it, not less."

142. My Cid Ruy Díaz stared at Pedro Bermúdez:
"Speak, Pedro Who Mute Is, you that are so silent!
To me they are daughters, to you first cousins;
when *I* am insulted, *you* get the slap in the face.
If I do the answering, you won't get to take up arms."

143. Pedro Bermúdez began to speak;
he was tonguetied and couldn't get his words out,
but I'll have you know, when once he got started there was no stopping him:
"Really, Cid, what ways you have about you!
Whenever we're in an assembly, you call me Pedro Who Mute Is!
You're well aware that I can't help it;
but what I have to do, I will accomplish without fail.
Fernando, every word you said was a lie;
your kinship with the Champion improved the standing of both of you greatly.
I can readily tell you personally what you're really like:
Remember when we were fighting outside mighty Valencia?
You asked the loyal Champion's permission to lead the charge,
you sighted a Moor, you went to try your hand with him;
but you fled before you reached him.
If I hadn't helped, the Moor would have dealt hardly with you;
I rode past you and closed with the Moor,
defeating him with my first blows;
I gave you his horse, I kept it all a secret for your sake:
up till today I've revealed it to no one.
In the presence of My Cid and everyone else, you went and boasted
that you had killed the Moor, performing a deed of valor;
everyone believed you, but didn't know the truth.
Yes, you're good-looking, but a coward!
Tongue without hands, how do you dare speak?

144. Tell me, Fernando, grant me this assertion:

"¿non te viene en miente en Valençia lo del león,
"quando durmié mio Çid y el león se desató?
"E tú, Ferrando, ¿qué fizist con el pavor?
"¡metístet tras el escaño de mio Çid el Campeador!
"metístet, Ferrando, por o menos vales oy.
"Nós çercamos el escaño por curiar nuestro señor,
"fasta do despertó mio Çid, el que Valençia gañó;
"levantós del escaño e *f*os poral león;
"el león premió la cabeça, a mio Çid esperó,
"dexósle prender al cuello, e a la red le metió.
"Quando se tornó el buen Campeador,
"a sos vassallos víolos aderredor;
"demandó por *s*os yernos, ¡ninguno non falló!
"Riébtot el cuerpo por malo e por traidor.
"Éstot lidiaré aquí ante rey don Alfons
"por fijas del Çid, don Elvira e doña Sol:
"por quanto las dexastes menos valedes vos;
"ellas son mugieres e vos sodes varones,
"en todas guisas más valen que vos.
"Quando f*o*re la lid, si ploguiere al Criador,
"tú lo otorgarás a guisa de traydor;
"de quanto he dicho verdadero seré yo."
D' aquestos amos aquí quedó la razón.
145. Dí*a*g Gonçálv*e*z odredes lo que dixo:
"De natura somos de los co*m*des más li*n*pios;
"¡estos casamientos non fuessen apareçidos,
"por consagrar con mio Çid don Rodrigo!
"Porque dexamos sus fijas aun no nos repentimos;
"mientra que bivan pueden aver sospiros:
"lo que les fiziemos se*e*r les ha retraydo.
"Esto lidiaré a tod el más ardido:
"que por que las dexamos ondrados somos *nos mismos*."
146. Martín Antolínez en pie se *f*o levantar;
"¡Calla, alevoso, boca sin verdad!
"Lo del león no se te deve olbidar;
"saliste por la puerta, metístet al corral,
"fústed meter tras la viga lagar;
"más non vesti*st* el manto nin el brial.
"Yollo lidiaré, non passará por al:
"fijas del Çid, por que las vos dexastes,
"en todas guisas, sabed, que más que vos valen.

Don't you recall that incident with the lion in Valencia,
when My Cid was sleeping and the lion got loose?
You, Fernando, what did you do in your fear?
You hid under My Cid Champion's bench!
Fernando, you put yourself in a place that destroyed your reputation.
We approached the bench to guard our master
until My Cid, the conqueror of Valencia, awoke;
he rose from the bench and headed for the lion;
the lion lowered its head as it awaited My Cid;
it let itself be grasped by the neck, and he put it in its cage.
When the good Champion came back in,
he saw his vassals standing all around;
he asked where his sons-in-law were, but neither one was to be found!
I challenge you to mortal combat as being wicked and treacherous.
I shall uphold that challenge here before King Alfonso
in the name of the Cid's daughters Doña Elvira and Doña Sol:
when you two abandoned them, you forfeited your honor;
they are women and you are men,
but in every way they are better than you.
When the combat takes place, if it please the Creator,
you will confess your treachery,
and all I have said will be proved correct."
The dialogue between those two ended there.

145. Diego González spoke (you shall hear what he said):
"Our lineage as counts is of the purest;
I wish those marriages had never been initiated—
allying ourselves with My Cid Don Rodrigo!
We still don't regret deserting his daughters;
they may sigh over it as long as they live:
what we did will remain a reproach against them.
I shall uphold this in combat against the most daring man:
we ourselves gained honor by abandoning them."

146. Martín Antolínez stood up:
"Silence, perfidious man, mouth without truth!
No one must forget what you did when the lion escaped;
you went out the door, you entered the yard,
and hid behind the beam of the wine press;
you never wore that cape or tunic again.
I shall combat you without fail:
the Cid's daughters, whom you abandoned,
are worth more than you in every way, I tell you.

"Al partir de la lid por tu boca lo dirás,
"que eres traydor e mintist de quanto dicho has."

[**Tiradas 150–152** (versos 3508–3730):]
150. El rey alçó la mano, la cara se santigó;
"Yo lo juro par sant Esidre el de León
"que en todas nuestras tierras non ha tan buen varón."
Mio Çid en el cavallo, adelant se llegó,
fo besar la mano a so señor Alfons;
"Mandástesme mover a Bavieca al corredor,
"en moros ni en cristianos otro tal non ha oy,
"yo vos le do en don, mandédesle tomar, señor."
Essora dixo el rey: "Desto non he sabor;
"si a vos le tolliés, el cavallo no havrié tan buen señor.
"Mas atal cavallo cum ést pora tal commo vos,
"pora arrancar moros del canpo e seer segudador;
"quien vos lo toller quisiere nol vala el Criador,
"ca por vos e por el cavallo ondrados somo' nos."
Essora se espidieron, e luégos partió la cort.
El Campeador a los que han lidiar tan bien los castigó:
"Ya Martín Antolínez, e vos, Per Vermudoz,
"e Muño Gustioz, *mio vassallo de pro,*
firmes seed en campo a guisa de varones;
"buenos mandados me vayan a Valençia de vos."

When the combat is over, you'll say as much yourself:
that you're treacherous and that everything you said was a lie."

[SUMMARY of strophes **147–149** (verses 3372–3507): Ansur González
arrives, flushed from a heavy meal, and insults the Cid as being a
common miller. He is challenged in his turn by Muño Gustioz. At that
moment two knights enter the assembly, one sent by the crown prince
of Navarre, the other by the crown prince of Aragon, who are asking
for the Cid's daughters in marriage. Again the Cid leaves the matter
to the king, who approves, and the emissaries give their pledge. Álvar
Fáñez speaks out, gloating that now the lords of Carrión will of ne-
cessity look up to the Cid's daughters. The king orders the judicial
combats for the next day, but the young lords of Carrión get a three
weeks' postponement and a change of venue to Carrión. The Cid re-
leases his three challengers into the king's charge; he himself must
return to Valencia. On taking leave, he lets his beard fall freely. He re-
turns the king's two hundred marks. (At this point, yet another MS
folio is missing. Apparently the king requests that, before leaving, the
Cid give him a demonstration of his horse Babieca's excellence.)]

[**Strophes 150–152** (verses 3508–3730):]

150. The king raised his hand and made the sign of the cross in front of his face:
"I swear by Saint Isidore of León
that in all our lands there is no other man as capable."
My Cid rode forward on his horse
and kissed his lord Alfonso's hand:
"You ordered me to show you swift Babieca's paces;
there is no other such horse today among Moors or Christians;
I make you a present of him; please accept him, sire."
Then the king said: "I do not wish to;
if I took him away from you, the horse wouldn't have so good a master.
A horse as fine as he is belongs with a man like you,
to vanquish Moors in battle and pursue them afterward;
may the Creator not protect anyone who wished to take him from you!
For we gain honor by you and by that steed."
Then they parted, and at once the assembly was dissolved.
The Champion gave good advice to those who were to fight:
"O Martín Antolínez, and you, Pedro Bermúdez,
and Muño Gustioz, my excellent vassal,
be steadfast in the field like brave men;
let good reports of you come to Valencia."

Dixo Martín Antolínez: "¿Por qué lo dezides, señor!
"Preso avemos el debdo e a passar es por nos;
"podedes odir de muertos, ca de vencidos no."
Alegre fo d' aquesto el que en buen ora nació;
espidiós de todos los que sos amigos son.
Mio Çid pora Valencia, e el rey pora Carrión.
Mas tres sedmanas de plazo todas complidas son.
Felos al plazdo los del Campeador,
cunplir quieren el debdo que les mandó so señor;
ellos son en poder de Alfons el de León;
dos días atendieron a ifantes de Carrión.
Mucho vienen bien adobados de cavallos e de guarnizones;
e todos sos parientes con ellos *acordados* son
que si los pudiessen apartar a los del Campeador,
que los matassen en campo por desondra de so señor.
El cometer fue malo, que lo al nos enpeçó,
ca grand miedo ovieron a Alfonsso el de León.
De noche belaron las armas e rogaron al Criador.
Troçida es la noche, ya crieban los albores;
muchos se juntaron de buenos ricos omnes
por veer esta lid, ca avién ende sabor;
demás sobre todos i es el rey don Alfons,
por querer el derecho e *ningun* tuerto non.
Yas metién en armas los del buen Campeador,
todos tres se acuerdan, ca son de un señor.
En otro logar se arman ifantes de Carrión;
sediélos castigando el comde Garçi Ordóñez.
Andidieron en pleyto, dixiéronle al rey Alfons,
que non fossen en la batalla Colada e Tizón,
que non lidiassen con ellas los del Canpeador;
mucho eran repentidos los ifantes por quanto dadas son.
Dixiérongelo al rey, mas non gelo conloyó;
"Non sacastes ninguna quando oviemos la cort.
"Si buenas las tenedes, pro abrán a vos;
"otrosí farán a los del Canpeador.
"Levad e salid al campo, ifantes de Carrión,
"huebos vos es que lidiedes, a guisa de varones,
"que nada non mancará por los del Campeador.
"Si del campo bien salides, grand ondra avredes vos;
"e ssi fuéredes vençidos, non rebtedes a nos,
"ca todos lo saben que lo buscastes vos."

Martín Antolínez said: "Why do you remind us, lord?
We have undertaken the obligation and it is incumbent on us;
you may hear that we're dead, but not that we were defeated."
The man born in a lucky hour was pleased by this;
he took leave of all who were his friends.
My Cid set out for Valencia, the king to Carrión.
Now the three weeks to the appointed day have elapsed.
Behold the Champion's men at the venue,
eager to carry out the duty their lord had imposed upon them;
they were under the protection of Alfonso of León;
for two days they awaited the young lords of Carrión.
They arrived very well equipped with horses and armor;
and all their kinsmen had planned together with them
that, if they could isolate the Champion's men,
they would kill them in the field to their lord's dishonor.
The scheme was evil, but wasn't put into action
because they greatly feared Alfonso of León.
At night they held a vigil of arms and prayed to the Creator.
The night had gone by, the dawn was just breaking;
numerous worthy noblemen assembled
to see that combat, because it appealed to them;
first and foremost among them was King Alfonso,
because he cherished justice and opposed wrongdoing.
Now the good Champion's men donned their armor,
all three of one mind, because they served one lord.
In another place the young lords of Carrión armed themselves
and received instructions from Count Garci Ordóñez.
They went with a petition, addressed to King Alfonso,
that Colada and Tizona should not be used in the combat,
that the Champion's men should not fight with them;
the young lords much regretted having returned them.
They asked this of the king, but he didn't consent:
"When we held the assembly, you didn't exclude any sword.
If you have good swords, they will be of service to you;
the same holds for the Champion's men.
Rise and go out to the field, young lords of Carrión,
you must fight like men,
for the Champion's vassals will do their utmost.
If you emerge victorious, you will gain great honor,
but if you are defeated, don't blame us,
because everyone knows you caused it all."

Ya se van repintiendo ifantes de Carrión,
de lo que avién fecho muchos repisos son;
no lo querrién aver fecho por quanto ha en Carrión.
Todos tres son armados los del Campeador,
ívalos veer el rey don Alfons.
Essora le dixieron los del Campeador:
"Besámosvos las manos commo a rey e a señor,
"que fidel seades oy dellos e de nos;
"a derecho nos valed, a ningun tuerto no.
"Aquí tienen so vando ifantes de Carrión,
"non sabemos qués comidrán ellos o qué non;
"en vuestra mano nos metió nuestro señor;
"tenendos a derecho, ¡por amor del Criador!"
Essora dixo el rey: "d' alma e de coraçón."
Adúzenles los cavallos buenos e corredores,
santiguaron las siellas e cavalgan a vigor;
los escudos a los cuellos que bien blocados son;
e' mano prenden las astas de los fierros tajadores,
estas tres lanças traen seños pendones;
e derredor dellos muchos buenos varones.
Ya salieron al campo do eran los mojones.
Todos tres son acordados los del Campeadore,
que cada uno dellos bien fos ferir el sove.
Fevos de la otra part ifantes de Carrione,
muy bien aconpañados, ca muchos parientes sone.
El rey dioles fideles por dezir el derecho e al none;
que non varagen con ellos de sí o de none.
Do sedién en el campo fabló rey don Alfonsse:
"Oíd que vos digo, ifantes de Carrione:
"esta lid en Toledo la fiziérades, mas non quisiestes vose.
"Estos tres cavalleros de mio Çid el Campeadore
"yo los adux a salvo a tierras de Carrione.
"Aved vuestro derecho, tuerto non querades vose,
"ca qui tuerto quisiere fazer, mal gelo vedaré yove,
"en todo myo reyno non avrá buena sabore."
Ya les va pesando a ifantes de Carrione.
Los fideles y el rey enseñaron los mojones,
librávanse del campo todos a derredor.
Bien gelo demostraron a todos seys commo son,
que por i serié vençido qui saliesse del mojón.
Todas las yentes esconbraron a derredor,

Now the young lords of Carrión were sorry,
greatly regretting what they had done;
they'd give all the wealth in Carrión not to have done it.
All three of the Champion's men were already armed
when they were visited by King Alfonso.
Then the Champion's men said to him:
"We kiss your hands as our king and lord;
be an impartial arbiter of both sides today;
protect us in the name of justice, see that no harm comes to us.
The young lords of Carrión have their whole faction here,
and we don't know what they will or won't contrive;
our master placed us in your hands;
sustain us justly, for the Creator's sake!"
Then the king said: "With heart and soul!"
Their good, swift horses were brought;
they made the sign of the cross over the saddles and mounted rapidly;
their strong-bossed shields hanging behind their necks,
they grasped the shafts of their sharp lances,
each of which bore a pennant;
around them were many good men.
Now they rode out to the field where the boundary markers stood.
All three of the Champion's men agreed
that each of them would strike his opponent powerfully.
Behold on the other side the young lords of Carrión,
with a large escort of numerous kinsmen.
The king appointed umpires to maintain strict justice
and keep them from disputing about right or wrong.
When they were in the field, King Alfonso spoke:
"Hear what I say to you, young lords of Carrión:
you could have fought this battle in Toledo, but you refused.
These three knights of My Cid the Champion
came to the lands of Carrión under my protection.
Uphold justice, seek no wrongdoing,
for if any man tries to do wrong, I shall impede it with severity;
he shall be out of favor throughout my kingdom."
Now the young lords of Carrión were grieved.
The umpires and the king pointed out the boundary markers,
and everyone round about departed from the field.
All six combatants were informed very clearly
that anyone passing the boundaries would count as defeated.
Everybody left a clear space all around,

de seys astas de lanças que non llegassen al mojón.
Sorteávanles el campo, ya les partién el sol,
salién los fideles de medio, ellos cara por cara son;
desí vienen los de mio Çid a ifantes de Carrión,
e ifantes de Carrión a los del Campeador;
cada uno dellos mientes tiene al so.
Abraçan los escudos delant los coraçones,
abaxan las lanças abueltas con los pendones,
enclinavan las caras sobre los arzones,
batién los cavallos con los espolones,
tembrar querié la tierra dond eran movedores.
Cada uno dellos mientes tiénet al so;
todos tres por tres ya juntados son:
cuédanse que essora cadrán muertos los que están aderredor.
Per Vermudoz, el que antes rebtó,
con Ferránt Gonçalvez de cara se juntó;
firiénsse en los escudos sin todo pavor.
Ferrán Gonçalvez a don Pero el escudol passó,
prísol en vázio, en carne nol tomó,
bien en dos logares el astil le quebró.
Firme estido Per Vermudoz, por esso nos encamó;
un colpe reçibiera, mas otro firió:
crebantó la bloca del escudo, apart gela echó,
passógelo todo, que nada nol valió.
Metiól la lança por los pechos, çerca del coraçón;
tres dobles de loriga tenié Fernando, aquestol prestó,
las dos le desmanchan e la terçera fincó:
el belmez con la camisa e con la guarnizón
de dentro en la carne una mano gela metió;
por la boca afuera la sángrel salió;
crebáronle las çinchas, ninguna nol ovo pro,
por la copla del cavallo en tierra lo echó.
Assí lo tenién las yentes que mal ferido es de muort.
En elle dexó la lança e mano al espada metió,
quando lo vido Ferrán Gonçalvez, conuvo a Tizón;
antes que el colpe esperasse dixo: "vençudo so".
Atorgaróngelo los fideles, Per Vermudoz le dexó.
151. Don Martino e Díag Gonçalvez firiéronse de las lanças,
tales foron los colpes que les crebaron amas.
Martín Antolínez mano metió al espada,
relumbra tod el campo, tanto es linpia e clara;

not being allowed to come within six lance-lengths of the boundary.
The sides of the field were assigned by lot, and the sunlight was evenly distributed;
the umpires left the center and the combatants were face to face;
Then My Cid's men approached the young lords of Carrión,
and the young lords of Carrión the Champion's men;
each of them was intent on his own opponent.
They gripped their shields and covered their hearts,
they lowered their pennanted lances,
bent their faces over their saddletrees,
and pricked their horses with their large spurs;
the ground shook when they rode forth.
Each of them concentrated on his own foe;
the three pairs were now in close combat:
those standing around thought they would now fall dead.
Pedro Bermúdez, who had issued his challenge first,
came to grips with Fernán González;
they struck each other's shields fearlessly.
Fernán González pierced Don Pedro's shield,
but his lance fell short, not reaching his flesh;
his shaft broke in two places.
Pedro Bermúdez sat his horse firmly, not wavering;
he had received one blow, but he struck another:
he shattered the boss of his enemy's shield, breaking it apart,
and pierced right through the shield, which offered no protection.
He thrust his lance into his chest, near the heart;
Fernando was wearing three-layered mail, which helped him;
two layers were torn apart but the third held fast:
his tunic, shirt, and armor
entered his flesh to the depth of a span;
blood gushed from his mouth;
his girths split, none of them was good any more,
and he tumbled to the ground over his horse's crupper.
Everyone thought he had been wounded mortally.
Don Pedro left his lance in him and drew his sword;
when Fernán González saw it, he recognized Tizona;
not waiting for the blow to fall, he shouted: "I am defeated!"
The umpires consented, and Pedro Bermúdez withdrew.
151. Don Martín and Diego González struck each other with their lances;
the blows were so great that both lances broke.
Martín Antolínez drew his sword,
which was so clean and bright, it illuminated the whole field;

diol un colpe, de traviéssol tomava:
el casco de somo apart gelo echava,
las moncluras del yelmo todas gelas cortava,
allá levó el almófar, fata la cofia llegava,
la cofia e el almófar todo gelo levava,
ráxol los pelos de la cabeça, bien a la carne llegava;
lo uno cayó en el campo e lo al suso fincava.
Quando este colpe a ferido Colada la preçiada,
vido Díag Gonçalvez que no escaparié con el alma;
bolvió la rienda al cavallo por tornasse de cara,
espada tiene en mano mas no la ensayava.
Essora Martín Antolínez reçibiól con el espada,
un cólpel dio de llano, con lo agudo nol tomava.
Essora el ifante tan grandes vozes dava:
"¡valme, Dios glorioso, señor, cúriam deste espada!"
el cavallo asorrienda, e mesurándol del espada,
sacól del mojón; don Martino en el campo fincava.
Essora dixo el rey: "venid vos a mi compaña;
"por quanto avedes fecho vençida avedes esta batalla."
Otórgangelo los fideles que dize verdadera palabra.
152. Los dos han arrancado; dirévos de Muño Gustioz,
con Anssuor Gonçálvez cómmo se adobó.
Firiénsse en los escudos unos tan grandes colpes.
Anssuor Gonçálvez, forçudo e de valor,
firió en el escudo a don Muño Gustioz,
tras el escudo falssóle la guarnizón;
en vázio fue la lança, ca en carne nol tomó.
Este colpe fecho, otro dio Muño Gustioz:
por medio de la bloca el escúdol crebantó;
nol pudo guarir, falssóle la guarnizón,
apart le priso, que non cab el coraçón;
metiól por la carne adentro la lança con el pendón,
de la otra part una braça gela echó,
con él dio una tuerta, de la siella lo encamó,
al tirar de la lança en tierra lo echó;
vermejo salió el astil, e la lança y el pendón.
Todos se cuedan que ferido es de muort.
La lança recombró e sobrél se paró;
dixo Gonçalvo Anssuórez: "¡nol firgades, por Dios!
"¡vençudo es el campo, quando esto se acabó!"
Dixieron los fideles: "esto odimos nos".

he dealt a blow—taking his foe crosswise—
which split apart the top of his helmet,
cutting through all its straps;
then it severed his mail cap and reached his cloth cap,
thrusting aside the cloth cap and the whole mail cap;
it scraped away the hair on his head and cut into the flesh;
part of his scalp fell to the ground, the rest remaining on his head.
After esteemed Colada had struck that blow,
Diego González saw that he wouldn't escape with his life;
he turned his horse around to flee,
holding his sword but not using it.
Then Martín Antolínez reached him with his sword,
striking him with the flat of it, not with its edge.
Then the young lord shouted loudly:
"Save me, glorious God my Lord, protect me from that sword!"
He pulled in his horse and, avoiding the sword,
rode past the boundary; Don Martín remained in the combat area.
Then the king said: "Come over to my group;
by what you have done, you have won this fight."
The umpires agreed that he had spoken a true word.
152. Those two have won; now I shall tell you about Muño Gustioz
and how he fared with Ansur González.
They struck several mighty blows at each other's shields.
Ansur González, strong and brave,
struck Don Muño Gustioz's shield,
piercing his armor behind the shield;
the lance fell short, it didn't reach his flesh.
When that blow had been struck, Muño Gustioz returned it:
he broke his foe's shield in the middle of the boss;
it couldn't protect him, his armor was pierced;
he was struck in the side, not near his heart;
the lance and its pennant entered his flesh
and six feet of it came out on the other side;
making a circular motion with the lance, he dislodged him from his saddle;
on pulling out the lance, he threw him to the ground;
the shaft emerged all red, as did the point and the pennant.
Everyone thought he was mortally wounded.
Muño recovered his lance and loomed over him;
Gonzalo Ansúrez shouted: "Don't strike him, for the love of God!
The field is won, now that this fight is over!"
The umpires said: "We hear and agree."

Mandó librar el canpo el buen rey don Alfons,
las armas que i rastaron el*le* se las tomó.
Por ondrados se parten los del buen Campeador;
vençieron esta lid, grado al Criador.
Grandes son los pesares por tierras de Carrión.
El rey a los de mio Çid de noche los enbió,
que no les diessen salto nin oviessen pavor.
A guisa de menbrados andan días e noches,
felos en Valençia con mio Çid el Campeador,
por malos los dexaron a ifantes de Carrión,
conplido han el debdo que les mandó so señor;
alegre fo d' aquesto mio Çid el Campeador.
Grant es la biltança de ifantes de Carrión.
Qui buena dueña escarneçe e la dexa despuós,
atal le contesca o siquier peor.
Dexémonos de pleitos de ifantes de Carrión,
de lo que an preso mucho an mal sabor;
fablemos nos d' aqueste que en buen ora naçió.
Grandes son los gozos en Valençia la mayor,
porque tan ondrados foron los del Canpeador.
Prísos a la barba Roy Díaz so señor:
"¡Grado al rey del çielo, mis fijas vengadas son!
"Agora las ayan quitas heredades de Carrión!
"Sin vergüença las casaré o a qui pese o a qui non."
Andidieron en pleytos los de Navarra e de Aragón,
ovieron su ajunta con Alfons el de León.
Fizieron *sos* casamientos don Elvira e doña Sol;
los primeros foron grandes, mas aquestos son mijores;
a mayor ondra las casa que lo que primero fo.
Ve*e*d qual ondra creçe al que en buen ora naçió,
quando señoras son su*e*s fijas de Navarra e de Aragón.
Oy los reyes dEspaña sos parientes son,
todos alcança ondra por el que en buen*a* naçió.
Passado es deste sieglo *mio Çid de Valençia señor*
el día de cinquaesma; ¡de Cristus aya perdón!
¡Assí ffagamos nós todos justos e peccadores!
Estas son las nuevas de mio Çid el Canpeador;
en este logar se acaba esta razón.

Good King Alfonso had the field cleared,
and took possession of the arms that had remained there.
The good Champion's men left the field with honor;
they had won that combat, thanks to the Creator.
Great was the vexation throughout the lands of Carrión.
The king sent off my Cid's men at night,
so they wouldn't be attacked or feel afraid.
As the prudent men they were, they journeyed days and nights:
behold them in Valencia with My Cid the Champion;
they had left the young lords of Carrión branded as villains,
they had fulfilled the obligation imposed by their master;
My Cid the Champion was pleased by this.
Great was the disgrace of the young lords of Carrión.
May any man who shames a good woman, and then deserts her,
meet up with this, or even worse!
Let us now leave the topic of the young lords of Carrión,
who were very unhappy with the treatment they received;
now let us speak of the man born in a lucky hour.
Great was the joy in mighty Valencia
because the Champion's men came off with such honor.
Ruy Díaz, their master, clutched his beard:
"Thanks to the king of heaven, my daughters are avenged!
Now they can say good riddance to their estates in Carrión!
Without cause for shame I shall marry them off, no matter what anyone says."
Those of Navarre and Aragon came to negotiate marriage,
meeting with Alfonso of León.
Doña Elvira and Doña Sol were married;
if their first marriages were distinguished, these were even more so;
he gave them higher-ranking husbands than they had had previously.
See the increase in honor of the man born in a lucky hour:
his daughters were rulers of Navarre and Aragon!
Today the kings of Spain are his descendants,
all deriving honor from the man born in a lucky hour.
My Cid, lord of Valencia, departed this life
on Pentecost Sunday. May he enjoy Christ's mercy!
So may we all, the just and the sinners alike!
This is the story of My Cid the Champion;
here this narrative ends.[36]

---

36. On the five further verses in the MS, see the Introduction.

A CATALOG OF SELECTED
DOVER BOOKS
IN ALL FIELDS OF INTEREST

A CATALOG OF SELECTED DOVER
BOOKS IN ALL FIELDS OF INTEREST

CONCERNING THE SPIRITUAL IN ART, Wassily Kandinsky. Pioneering work by father of abstract art. Thoughts on color theory, nature of art. Analysis of earlier masters. 12 illustrations. 80pp. of text. 5⅜ x 8½.   23411-8

ANIMALS: 1,419 Copyright-Free Illustrations of Mammals, Birds, Fish, Insects, etc., Jim Harter (ed.). Clear wood engravings present, in extremely lifelike poses, over 1,000 species of animals. One of the most extensive pictorial sourcebooks of its kind. Captions. Index. 284pp. 9 x 12.   23766-4

CELTIC ART: The Methods of Construction, George Bain. Simple geometric techniques for making Celtic interlacements, spirals, Kells-type initials, animals, humans, etc. Over 500 illustrations. 160pp. 9 x 12. (Available in U.S. only.)   22923-8

AN ATLAS OF ANATOMY FOR ARTISTS, Fritz Schider. Most thorough reference work on art anatomy in the world. Hundreds of illustrations, including selections from works by Vesalius, Leonardo, Goya, Ingres, Michelangelo, others. 593 illustrations. 192pp. 7⅛ x 10¼.   20241-0

CELTIC HAND STROKE-BY-STROKE (Irish Half-Uncial from "The Book of Kells"): An Arthur Baker Calligraphy Manual, Arthur Baker. Complete guide to creating each letter of the alphabet in distinctive Celtic manner. Covers hand position, strokes, pens, inks, paper, more. Illustrated. 48pp. 8¼ x 11.   24336-2

EASY ORIGAMI, John Montroll. Charming collection of 32 projects (hat, cup, pelican, piano, swan, many more) specially designed for the novice origami hobbyist. Clearly illustrated easy-to-follow instructions insure that even beginning papercrafters will achieve successful results. 48pp. 8¼ x 11.   27298-2

THE COMPLETE BOOK OF BIRDHOUSE CONSTRUCTION FOR WOODWORKERS, Scott D. Campbell. Detailed instructions, illustrations, tables. Also data on bird habitat and instinct patterns. Bibliography. 3 tables. 63 illustrations in 15 figures. 48pp. 5¼ x 8½.   24407-5

BLOOMINGDALE'S ILLUSTRATED 1886 CATALOG: Fashions, Dry Goods and Housewares, Bloomingdale Brothers. Famed merchants' extremely rare catalog depicting about 1,700 products: clothing, housewares, firearms, dry goods, jewelry, more. Invaluable for dating, identifying vintage items. Also, copyright-free graphics for artists, designers. Co-published with Henry Ford Museum & Greenfield Village. 160pp. 8¼ x 11.   25780-0

HISTORIC COSTUME IN PICTURES, Braun & Schneider. Over 1,450 costumed figures in clearly detailed engravings–from dawn of civilization to end of 19th century. Captions. Many folk costumes. 256pp. 8⅜ x 11¾.   23150-X

STICKLEY CRAFTSMAN FURNITURE CATALOGS, Gustav Stickley and L. & J. G. Stickley. Beautiful, functional furniture in two authentic catalogs from 1910. 594 illustrations, including 277 photos, show settles, rockers, armchairs, reclining chairs, bookcases, desks, tables. 183pp. 6½ x 9¼.   23838-5

AMERICAN LOCOMOTIVES IN HISTORIC PHOTOGRAPHS: 1858 to 1949, Ron Ziel (ed.). A rare collection of 126 meticulously detailed official photographs, called "builder portraits," of American locomotives that majestically chronicle the rise of steam locomotive power in America. Introduction. Detailed captions. xi+ 129pp. 9 x 12.   27393-8

AMERICA'S LIGHTHOUSES: An Illustrated History, Francis Ross Holland, Jr. Delightfully written, profusely illustrated fact-filled survey of over 200 American lighthouses since 1716. History, anecdotes, technological advances, more. 240pp. 8 x 10¾.
25576-X

TOWARDS A NEW ARCHITECTURE, Le Corbusier. Pioneering manifesto by founder of "International School." Technical and aesthetic theories, views of industry, economics, relation of form to function, "mass-production split" and much more. Profusely illustrated. 320pp. 6⅛ x 9¼. (Available in U.S. only.)   25023-7

HOW THE OTHER HALF LIVES, Jacob Riis. Famous journalistic record, exposing poverty and degradation of New York slums around 1900, by major social reformer. 100 striking and influential photographs. 233pp. 10 x 7⅞.   22012-5

FRUIT KEY AND TWIG KEY TO TREES AND SHRUBS, William M. Harlow. One of the handiest and most widely used identification aids. Fruit key covers 120 deciduous and evergreen species; twig key 160 deciduous species. Easily used. Over 300 photographs. 126pp. 5⅜ x 8½.   20511-8

COMMON BIRD SONGS, Dr. Donald J. Borror. Songs of 60 most common U.S. birds: robins, sparrows, cardinals, bluejays, finches, more—arranged in order of increasing complexity. Up to 9 variations of songs of each species.
Cassette and manual 99911-4

ORCHIDS AS HOUSE PLANTS, Rebecca Tyson Northen. Grow cattleyas and many other kinds of orchids—in a window, in a case, or under artificial light. 63 illustrations. 148pp. 5⅜ x 8½.   23261-1

MONSTER MAZES, Dave Phillips. Masterful mazes at four levels of difficulty. Avoid deadly perils and evil creatures to find magical treasures. Solutions for all 32 exciting illustrated puzzles. 48pp. 8¼ x 11.   26005-4

MOZART'S DON GIOVANNI (DOVER OPERA LIBRETTO SERIES), Wolfgang Amadeus Mozart. Introduced and translated by Ellen H. Bleiler. Standard Italian libretto, with complete English translation. Convenient and thoroughly portable—an ideal companion for reading along with a recording or the performance itself. Introduction. List of characters. Plot summary. 121pp. 5¼ x 8½.   24944-1

TECHNICAL MANUAL AND DICTIONARY OF CLASSICAL BALLET, Gail Grant. Defines, explains, comments on steps, movements, poses and concepts. 15-page pictorial section. Basic book for student, viewer. 127pp. 5⅜ x 8½.   21843-0

THE CLARINET AND CLARINET PLAYING, David Pino. Lively, comprehensive work features suggestions about technique, musicianship, and musical interpretation, as well as guidelines for teaching, making your own reeds, and preparing for public performance. Includes an intriguing look at clarinet history. "A godsend," *The Clarinet,* Journal of the International Clarinet Society. Appendixes. 7 illus. 320pp. 5⅜ x 8½. 40270-3

HOLLYWOOD GLAMOR PORTRAITS, John Kobal (ed.). 145 photos from 1926-49. Harlow, Gable, Bogart, Bacall; 94 stars in all. Full background on photographers, technical aspects. 160pp. 8⅜ x 11¼. 23352-9

THE ANNOTATED CASEY AT THE BAT: A Collection of Ballads about the Mighty Casey/Third, Revised Edition, Martin Gardner (ed.). Amusing sequels and parodies of one of America's best-loved poems: Casey's Revenge, Why Casey Whiffed, Casey's Sister at the Bat, others. 256pp. 5⅜ x 8½. 28598-7

THE RAVEN AND OTHER FAVORITE POEMS, Edgar Allan Poe. Over 40 of the author's most memorable poems: "The Bells," "Ulalume," "Israfel," "To Helen," "The Conqueror Worm," "Eldorado," "Annabel Lee," many more. Alphabetic lists of titles and first lines. 64pp. 5³⁄₁₆ x 8¼. 26685-0

PERSONAL MEMOIRS OF U. S. GRANT, Ulysses Simpson Grant. Intelligent, deeply moving firsthand account of Civil War campaigns, considered by many the finest military memoirs ever written. Includes letters, historic photographs, maps and more. 528pp. 6⅛ x 9¼. 28587-1

ANCIENT EGYPTIAN MATERIALS AND INDUSTRIES, A. Lucas and J. Harris. Fascinating, comprehensive, thoroughly documented text describes this ancient civilization's vast resources and the processes that incorporated them in daily life, including the use of animal products, building materials, cosmetics, perfumes and incense, fibers, glazed ware, glass and its manufacture, materials used in the mummification process, and much more. 544pp. 6¹⁄₈ x 9¹⁄₄. (Available in U.S. only.) 40446-3

RUSSIAN STORIES/RUSSKIE RASSKAZY: A Dual-Language Book, edited by Gleb Struve. Twelve tales by such masters as Chekhov, Tolstoy, Dostoevsky, Pushkin, others. Excellent word-for-word English translations on facing pages, plus teaching and study aids, Russian/English vocabulary, biographical/critical introductions, more. 416pp. 5⅜ x 8½. 26244-8

PHILADELPHIA THEN AND NOW: 60 Sites Photographed in the Past and Present, Kenneth Finkel and Susan Oyama. Rare photographs of City Hall, Logan Square, Independence Hall, Betsy Ross House, other landmarks juxtaposed with contemporary views. Captures changing face of historic city. Introduction. Captions. 128pp. 8¼ x 11. 25790-8

AIA ARCHITECTURAL GUIDE TO NASSAU AND SUFFOLK COUNTIES, LONG ISLAND, The American Institute of Architects, Long Island Chapter, and the Society for the Preservation of Long Island Antiquities. Comprehensive, well-researched and generously illustrated volume brings to life over three centuries of Long Island's great architectural heritage. More than 240 photographs with authoritative, extensively detailed captions. 176pp. 8¼ x 11. 26946-9

NORTH AMERICAN INDIAN LIFE: Customs and Traditions of 23 Tribes, Elsie Clews Parsons (ed.). 27 fictionalized essays by noted anthropologists examine religion, customs, government, additional facets of life among the Winnebago, Crow, Zuni, Eskimo, other tribes. 480pp. 6⅛ x 9¼. 27377-6

FRANK LLOYD WRIGHT'S DANA HOUSE, Donald Hoffmann. Pictorial essay of residential masterpiece with over 160 interior and exterior photos, plans, elevations, sketches and studies. 128pp. 9¼ x 10¾.   29120-0

THE MALE AND FEMALE FIGURE IN MOTION: 60 Classic Photographic Sequences, Eadweard Muybridge. 60 true-action photographs of men and women walking, running, climbing, bending, turning, etc., reproduced from rare 19th-century masterpiece. vi + 121pp. 9 x 12.   24745-7

1001 QUESTIONS ANSWERED ABOUT THE SEASHORE, N. J. Berrill and Jacquelyn Berrill. Queries answered about dolphins, sea snails, sponges, starfish, fishes, shore birds, many others. Covers appearance, breeding, growth, feeding, much more. 305pp. 5¼ x 8¼.   23366-9

ATTRACTING BIRDS TO YOUR YARD, William J. Weber. Easy-to-follow guide offers advice on how to attract the greatest diversity of birds: birdhouses, feeders, water and waterers, much more. 96pp. 5³⁄₁₆ x 8¼.   28927-3

MEDICINAL AND OTHER USES OF NORTH AMERICAN PLANTS: A Historical Survey with Special Reference to the Eastern Indian Tribes, Charlotte Erichsen-Brown. Chronological historical citations document 500 years of usage of plants, trees, shrubs native to eastern Canada, northeastern U.S. Also complete identifying information. 343 illustrations. 544pp. 6½ x 9¼.   25951-X

STORYBOOK MAZES, Dave Phillips. 23 stories and mazes on two-page spreads: Wizard of Oz, Treasure Island, Robin Hood, etc. Solutions. 64pp. 8¼ x 11. 23628-5

AMERICAN NEGRO SONGS: 230 Folk Songs and Spirituals, Religious and Secular, John W. Work. This authoritative study traces the African influences of songs sung and played by black Americans at work, in church, and as entertainment. The author discusses the lyric significance of such songs as "Swing Low, Sweet Chariot," "John Henry," and others and offers the words and music for 230 songs. Bibliography. Index of Song Titles. 272pp. 6½ x 9¼.   40271-1

MOVIE-STAR PORTRAITS OF THE FORTIES, John Kobal (ed.). 163 glamor, studio photos of 106 stars of the 1940s: Rita Hayworth, Ava Gardner, Marlon Brando, Clark Gable, many more. 176pp. 8⅜ x 11¼.   23546-7

BENCHLEY LOST AND FOUND, Robert Benchley. Finest humor from early 30s, about pet peeves, child psychologists, post office and others. Mostly unavailable elsewhere. 73 illustrations by Peter Arno and others. 183pp. 5⅜ x 8½. 22410-4

YEKL and THE IMPORTED BRIDEGROOM AND OTHER STORIES OF YIDDISH NEW YORK, Abraham Cahan. Film Hester Street based on *Yekl* (1896). Novel, other stories among first about Jewish immigrants on N.Y.'s East Side. 240pp. 5⅜ x 8½.   22427-9

SELECTED POEMS, Walt Whitman. Generous sampling from *Leaves of Grass*. Twenty-four poems include "I Hear America Singing," "Song of the Open Road," "I Sing the Body Electric," "When Lilacs Last in the Dooryard Bloom'd," "O Captain! My Captain!"–all reprinted from an authoritative edition. Lists of titles and first lines. 128pp. 5³⁄₁₆ x 8¼.   26878-0

THE BEST TALES OF HOFFMANN, E. T. A. Hoffmann. 10 of Hoffmann's most important stories: "Nutcracker and the King of Mice," "The Golden Flowerpot," etc. 458pp. 5⅜ x 8½. 21793-0

FROM FETISH TO GOD IN ANCIENT EGYPT, E. A. Wallis Budge. Rich detailed survey of Egyptian conception of "God" and gods, magic, cult of animals, Osiris, more. Also, superb English translations of hymns and legends. 240 illustrations. 545pp. 5⅜ x 8½. 25803-3

FRENCH STORIES/CONTES FRANÇAIS: A Dual-Language Book, Wallace Fowlie. Ten stories by French masters, Voltaire to Camus: "Micromegas" by Voltaire; "The Atheist's Mass" by Balzac; "Minuet" by de Maupassant; "The Guest" by Camus, six more. Excellent English translations on facing pages. Also French-English vocabulary list, exercises, more. 352pp. 5⅜ x 8½. 26443-2

CHICAGO AT THE TURN OF THE CENTURY IN PHOTOGRAPHS: 122 Historic Views from the Collections of the Chicago Historical Society, Larry A. Viskochil. Rare large-format prints offer detailed views of City Hall, State Street, the Loop, Hull House, Union Station, many other landmarks, circa 1904-1913. Introduction. Captions. Maps. 144pp. 9⅜ x 12¼. 24656-6

OLD BROOKLYN IN EARLY PHOTOGRAPHS, 1865-1929, William Lee Younger. Luna Park, Gravesend race track, construction of Grand Army Plaza, moving of Hotel Brighton, etc. 157 previously unpublished photographs. 165pp. 8⅞ x 11¾. 23587-4

THE MYTHS OF THE NORTH AMERICAN INDIANS, Lewis Spence. Rich anthology of the myths and legends of the Algonquins, Iroquois, Pawnees and Sioux, prefaced by an extensive historical and ethnological commentary. 36 illustrations. 480pp. 5⅜ x 8½. 25967-6

AN ENCYCLOPEDIA OF BATTLES: Accounts of Over 1,560 Battles from 1479 B.C. to the Present, David Eggenberger. Essential details of every major battle in recorded history from the first battle of Megiddo in 1479 B.C. to Grenada in 1984. List of Battle Maps. New Appendix covering the years 1967-1984. Index. 99 illustrations. 544pp. 6½ x 9¼. 24913-1

SAILING ALONE AROUND THE WORLD, Captain Joshua Slocum. First man to sail around the world, alone, in small boat. One of great feats of seamanship told in delightful manner. 67 illustrations. 294pp. 5⅜ x 8½. 20326-3

ANARCHISM AND OTHER ESSAYS, Emma Goldman. Powerful, penetrating, prophetic essays on direct action, role of minorities, prison reform, puritan hypocrisy, violence, etc. 271pp. 5⅜ x 8½. 22484-8

MYTHS OF THE HINDUS AND BUDDHISTS, Ananda K. Coomaraswamy and Sister Nivedita. Great stories of the epics; deeds of Krishna, Shiva, taken from puranas, Vedas, folk tales; etc. 32 illustrations. 400pp. 5⅜ x 8½. 21759-0

THE TRAUMA OF BIRTH, Otto Rank. Rank's controversial thesis that anxiety neurosis is caused by profound psychological trauma which occurs at birth. 256pp. 5⅜ x 8½. 27974-X

A THEOLOGICO-POLITICAL TREATISE, Benedict Spinoza. Also contains unfinished Political Treatise. Great classic on religious liberty, theory of government on common consent. R. Elwes translation. Total of 421pp. 5⅜ x 8½. 20249-6

MY BONDAGE AND MY FREEDOM, Frederick Douglass. Born a slave, Douglass became outspoken force in antislavery movement. The best of Douglass' autobiographies. Graphic description of slave life. 464pp. 5⅜ x 8½.   22457-0

FOLLOWING THE EQUATOR: A Journey Around the World, Mark Twain. Fascinating humorous account of 1897 voyage to Hawaii, Australia, India, New Zealand, etc. Ironic, bemused reports on peoples, customs, climate, flora and fauna, politics, much more. 197 illustrations. 720pp. 5⅜ x 8½.   26113-1

THE PEOPLE CALLED SHAKERS, Edward D. Andrews. Definitive study of Shakers: origins, beliefs, practices, dances, social organization, furniture and crafts, etc. 33 illustrations. 351pp. 5⅜ x 8½.   21081-2

THE MYTHS OF GREECE AND ROME, H. A. Guerber. A classic of mythology, generously illustrated, long prized for its simple, graphic, accurate retelling of the principal myths of Greece and Rome, and for its commentary on their origins and significance. With 64 illustrations by Michelangelo, Raphael, Titian, Rubens, Canova, Bernini and others. 480pp. 5⅜ x 8½.   27584-1

PSYCHOLOGY OF MUSIC, Carl E. Seashore. Classic work discusses music as a medium from psychological viewpoint. Clear treatment of physical acoustics, auditory apparatus, sound perception, development of musical skills, nature of musical feeling, host of other topics. 88 figures. 408pp. 5⅜ x 8½.   21851-1

THE PHILOSOPHY OF HISTORY, Georg W. Hegel. Great classic of Western thought develops concept that history is not chance but rational process, the evolution of freedom. 457pp. 5⅜ x 8½.   20112-0

THE BOOK OF TEA, Kakuzo Okakura. Minor classic of the Orient: entertaining, charming explanation, interpretation of traditional Japanese culture in terms of tea ceremony. 94pp. 5⅜ x 8½.   20070-1

LIFE IN ANCIENT EGYPT, Adolf Erman. Fullest, most thorough, detailed older account with much not in more recent books, domestic life, religion, magic, medicine, commerce, much more. Many illustrations reproduce tomb paintings, carvings, hieroglyphs, etc. 597pp. 5⅜ x 8½.   22632-8

SUNDIALS, Their Theory and Construction, Albert Waugh. Far and away the best, most thorough coverage of ideas, mathematics concerned, types, construction, adjusting anywhere. Simple, nontechnical treatment allows even children to build several of these dials. Over 100 illustrations. 230pp. 5⅜ x 8½.   22947-5

THEORETICAL HYDRODYNAMICS, L. M. Milne-Thomson. Classic exposition of the mathematical theory of fluid motion, applicable to both hydrodynamics and aerodynamics. Over 600 exercises. 768pp. 6⅛ x 9¼.   68970-0

SONGS OF EXPERIENCE: Facsimile Reproduction with 26 Plates in Full Color, William Blake. 26 full-color plates from a rare 1826 edition. Includes "The Tyger," "London," "Holy Thursday," and other poems. Printed text of poems. 48pp. 5¼ x 7.   24636-1

OLD-TIME VIGNETTES IN FULL COLOR, Carol Belanger Grafton (ed.). Over 390 charming, often sentimental illustrations, selected from archives of Victorian graphics—pretty women posing, children playing, food, flowers, kittens and puppies, smiling cherubs, birds and butterflies, much more. All copyright-free. 48pp. 9¼ x 12¼.   27269-9

PERSPECTIVE FOR ARTISTS, Rex Vicat Cole. Depth, perspective of sky and sea, shadows, much more, not usually covered. 391 diagrams, 81 reproductions of drawings and paintings. 279pp. $5\frac{3}{8}$ x $8\frac{1}{2}$. 22487-2

DRAWING THE LIVING FIGURE, Joseph Sheppard. Innovative approach to artistic anatomy focuses on specifics of surface anatomy, rather than muscles and bones. Over 170 drawings of live models in front, back and side views, and in widely varying poses. Accompanying diagrams. 177 illustrations. Introduction. Index. 144pp. $8\frac{3}{8}$ x$11\frac{1}{4}$. 26723-7

GOTHIC AND OLD ENGLISH ALPHABETS: 100 Complete Fonts, Dan X. Solo. Add power, elegance to posters, signs, other graphics with 100 stunning copyright-free alphabets: Blackstone, Dolbey, Germania, 97 more–including many lower-case, numerals, punctuation marks. 104pp. $8\frac{1}{8}$ x 11. 24695-7

HOW TO DO BEADWORK, Mary White. Fundamental book on craft from simple projects to five-bead chains and woven works. 106 illustrations. 142pp. $5\frac{3}{8}$ x 8. 20697-1

THE BOOK OF WOOD CARVING, Charles Marshall Sayers. Finest book for beginners discusses fundamentals and offers 34 designs. "Absolutely first rate . . . well thought out and well executed."–E. J. Tangerman. 118pp. $7\frac{3}{4}$ x $10\frac{5}{8}$. 23654-4

ILLUSTRATED CATALOG OF CIVIL WAR MILITARY GOODS: Union Army Weapons, Insignia, Uniform Accessories, and Other Equipment, Schuyler, Hartley, and Graham. Rare, profusely illustrated 1846 catalog includes Union Army uniform and dress regulations, arms and ammunition, coats, insignia, flags, swords, rifles, etc. 226 illustrations. 160pp. 9 x 12. 24939-5

WOMEN'S FASHIONS OF THE EARLY 1900s: An Unabridged Republication of "New York Fashions, 1909," National Cloak & Suit Co. Rare catalog of mail-order fashions documents women's and children's clothing styles shortly after the turn of the century. Captions offer full descriptions, prices. Invaluable resource for fashion, costume historians. Approximately 725 illustrations. 128pp. $8\frac{3}{8}$ x $11\frac{1}{4}$. 27276-1

THE 1912 AND 1915 GUSTAV STICKLEY FURNITURE CATALOGS, Gustav Stickley. With over 200 detailed illustrations and descriptions, these two catalogs are essential reading and reference materials and identification guides for Stickley furniture. Captions cite materials, dimensions and prices. 112pp. $6\frac{1}{2}$ x $9\frac{1}{4}$. 26676-1

EARLY AMERICAN LOCOMOTIVES, John H. White, Jr. Finest locomotive engravings from early 19th century: historical (1804–74), main-line (after 1870), special, foreign, etc. 147 plates. 142pp. $11\frac{3}{8}$ x $8\frac{1}{4}$. 22772-3

THE TALL SHIPS OF TODAY IN PHOTOGRAPHS, Frank O. Braynard. Lavishly illustrated tribute to nearly 100 majestic contemporary sailing vessels: Amerigo Vespucci, Clearwater, Constitution, Eagle, Mayflower, Sea Cloud, Victory, many more. Authoritative captions provide statistics, background on each ship. 190 black-and-white photographs and illustrations. Introduction. 128pp. $8\frac{7}{8}$ x $11\frac{3}{4}$. 27163-3

LITTLE BOOK OF EARLY AMERICAN CRAFTS AND TRADES, Peter Stockham (ed.). 1807 children's book explains crafts and trades: baker, hatter, cooper, potter, and many others. 23 copperplate illustrations. 140pp. 4⅝ x 6. 23336-7

VICTORIAN FASHIONS AND COSTUMES FROM HARPER'S BAZAR, 1867–1898, Stella Blum (ed.). Day costumes, evening wear, sports clothes, shoes, hats, other accessories in over 1,000 detailed engravings. 320pp. 9⅜ x 12¼. 22990-4

GUSTAV STICKLEY, THE CRAFTSMAN, Mary Ann Smith. Superb study surveys broad scope of Stickley's achievement, especially in architecture. Design philosophy, rise and fall of the Craftsman empire, descriptions and floor plans for many Craftsman houses, more. 86 black-and-white halftones. 31 line illustrations. Introduction 208pp. 6½ x 9¼. 27210-9

THE LONG ISLAND RAIL ROAD IN EARLY PHOTOGRAPHS, Ron Ziel. Over 220 rare photos, informative text document origin (1844) and development of rail service on Long Island. Vintage views of early trains, locomotives, stations, passengers, crews, much more. Captions. 8⅞ x 11¾. 26301-0

VOYAGE OF THE LIBERDADE, Joshua Slocum. Great 19th-century mariner's thrilling, first-hand account of the wreck of his ship off South America, the 35-foot boat he built from the wreckage, and its remarkable voyage home. 128pp. 5⅜ x 8½. 40022-0

TEN BOOKS ON ARCHITECTURE, Vitruvius. The most important book ever written on architecture. Early Roman aesthetics, technology, classical orders, site selection, all other aspects. Morgan translation. 331pp. 5⅜ x 8½. 20645-9

THE HUMAN FIGURE IN MOTION, Eadweard Muybridge. More than 4,500 stopped-action photos, in action series, showing undraped men, women, children jumping, lying down, throwing, sitting, wrestling, carrying, etc. 390pp. 7⅞ x 10⅝. 20204-6 Clothbd.

TREES OF THE EASTERN AND CENTRAL UNITED STATES AND CANADA, William M. Harlow. Best one-volume guide to 140 trees. Full descriptions, woodlore, range, etc. Over 600 illustrations. Handy size. 288pp. 4½ x 6⅜. 20395-6

SONGS OF WESTERN BIRDS, Dr. Donald J. Borror. Complete song and call repertoire of 60 western species, including flycatchers, juncoes, cactus wrens, many more—includes fully illustrated booklet. Cassette and manual 99913-0

GROWING AND USING HERBS AND SPICES, Milo Miloradovich. Versatile handbook provides all the information needed for cultivation and use of all the herbs and spices available in North America. 4 illustrations. Index. Glossary. 236pp. 5⅜ x 8½. 25058-X

BIG BOOK OF MAZES AND LABYRINTHS, Walter Shepherd. 50 mazes and labyrinths in all—classical, solid, ripple, and more—in one great volume. Perfect inexpensive puzzler for clever youngsters. Full solutions. 112pp. 8⅛ x 11. 22951-3

PIANO TUNING, J. Cree Fischer. Clearest, best book for beginner, amateur. Simple repairs, raising dropped notes, tuning by easy method of flattened fifths. No previous skills needed. 4 illustrations. 201pp. 5⅜ x 8½. 23267-0

HINTS TO SINGERS, Lillian Nordica. Selecting the right teacher, developing confidence, overcoming stage fright, and many other important skills receive thoughtful discussion in this indispensible guide, written by a world-famous diva of four decades' experience. 96pp. 5⅜ x 8½. 40094-8

THE COMPLETE NONSENSE OF EDWARD LEAR, Edward Lear. All nonsense limericks, zany alphabets, Owl and Pussycat, songs, nonsense botany, etc., illustrated by Lear. Total of 320pp. 5⅜ x 8½. (Available in U.S. only.) 20167-8

VICTORIAN PARLOUR POETRY: An Annotated Anthology, Michael R. Turner. 117 gems by Longfellow, Tennyson, Browning, many lesser-known poets. "The Village Blacksmith," "Curfew Must Not Ring Tonight," "Only a Baby Small," dozens more, often difficult to find elsewhere. Index of poets, titles, first lines. xxiii + 325pp. 5⅝ x 8¼. 27044-0

DUBLINERS, James Joyce. Fifteen stories offer vivid, tightly focused observations of the lives of Dublin's poorer classes. At least one, "The Dead," is considered a masterpiece. Reprinted complete and unabridged from standard edition. 160pp. 5$^{3}/_{16}$ x 8¼. 26870-5

GREAT WEIRD TALES: 14 Stories by Lovecraft, Blackwood, Machen and Others, S. T. Joshi (ed.). 14 spellbinding tales, including "The Sin Eater," by Fiona McLeod, "The Eye Above the Mantel," by Frank Belknap Long, as well as renowned works by R. H. Barlow, Lord Dunsany, Arthur Machen, W. C. Morrow and eight other masters of the genre. 256pp. 5⅜ x 8½. (Available in U.S. only.) 40436-6

THE BOOK OF THE SACRED MAGIC OF ABRAMELIN THE MAGE, translated by S. MacGregor Mathers. Medieval manuscript of ceremonial magic. Basic document in Aleister Crowley, Golden Dawn groups. 268pp. 5⅜ x 8½. 23211-5

NEW RUSSIAN-ENGLISH AND ENGLISH-RUSSIAN DICTIONARY, M. A. O'Brien. This is a remarkably handy Russian dictionary, containing a surprising amount of information, including over 70,000 entries. 366pp. 4½ x 6⅛. 20208-9

HISTORIC HOMES OF THE AMERICAN PRESIDENTS, Second, Revised Edition, Irvin Haas. A traveler's guide to American Presidential homes, most open to the public, depicting and describing homes occupied by every American President from George Washington to George Bush. With visiting hours, admission charges, travel routes. 175 photographs. Index. 160pp. 8¼ x 11. 26751-2

NEW YORK IN THE FORTIES, Andreas Feininger. 162 brilliant photographs by the well-known photographer, formerly with *Life* magazine. Commuters, shoppers, Times Square at night, much else from city at its peak. Captions by John von Hartz. 181pp. 9¼ x 10¾. 23585-8

INDIAN SIGN LANGUAGE, William Tomkins. Over 525 signs developed by Sioux and other tribes. Written instructions and diagrams. Also 290 pictographs. 111pp. 6⅛ x 9¼. 22029-X

ANATOMY: A Complete Guide for Artists, Joseph Sheppard. A master of figure drawing shows artists how to render human anatomy convincingly. Over 460 illustrations. 224pp. 8⅜ x 11¼. 27279-6

MEDIEVAL CALLIGRAPHY: Its History and Technique, Marc Drogin. Spirited history, comprehensive instruction manual covers 13 styles (ca. 4th century through 15th). Excellent photographs; directions for duplicating medieval techniques with modern tools. 224pp. 8⅜ x 11¼. 26142-5

DRIED FLOWERS: How to Prepare Them, Sarah Whitlock and Martha Rankin. Complete instructions on how to use silica gel, meal and borax, perlite aggregate, sand and borax, glycerine and water to create attractive permanent flower arrangements. 12 illustrations. 32pp. 5⅜ x 8½. 21802-3

EASY-TO-MAKE BIRD FEEDERS FOR WOODWORKERS, Scott D. Campbell. Detailed, simple-to-use guide for designing, constructing, caring for and using feeders. Text, illustrations for 12 classic and contemporary designs. 96pp. 5⅜ x 8½. 25847-5

SCOTTISH WONDER TALES FROM MYTH AND LEGEND, Donald A. Mackenzie. 16 lively tales tell of giants rumbling down mountainsides, of a magic wand that turns stone pillars into warriors, of gods and goddesses, evil hags, powerful forces and more. 240pp. 5⅜ x 8½. 29677-6

THE HISTORY OF UNDERCLOTHES, C. Willett Cunnington and Phyllis Cunnington. Fascinating, well-documented survey covering six centuries of English undergarments, enhanced with over 100 illustrations: 12th-century laced-up bodice, footed long drawers (1795), 19th-century bustles, 19th-century corsets for men, Victorian "bust improvers," much more. 272pp. 5⅝ x 8¼. 27124-2

ARTS AND CRAFTS FURNITURE: The Complete Brooks Catalog of 1912, Brooks Manufacturing Co. Photos and detailed descriptions of more than 150 now very collectible furniture designs from the Arts and Crafts movement depict davenports, settees, buffets, desks, tables, chairs, bedsteads, dressers and more, all built of solid, quarter-sawed oak. Invaluable for students and enthusiasts of antiques, Americana and the decorative arts. 80pp. 6½ x 9¼. 27471-3

WILBUR AND ORVILLE: A Biography of the Wright Brothers, Fred Howard. Definitive, crisply written study tells the full story of the brothers' lives and work. A vividly written biography, unparalleled in scope and color, that also captures the spirit of an extraordinary era. 560pp. 6⅛ x 9¼. 40297-5

THE ARTS OF THE SAILOR: Knotting, Splicing and Ropework, Hervey Garrett Smith. Indispensable shipboard reference covers tools, basic knots and useful hitches; handsewing and canvas work, more. Over 100 illustrations. Delightful reading for sea lovers. 256pp. 5⅜ x 8½. 26440-8

FRANK LLOYD WRIGHT'S FALLINGWATER: The House and Its History, Second, Revised Edition, Donald Hoffmann. A total revision–both in text and illustrations–of the standard document on Fallingwater, the boldest, most personal architectural statement of Wright's mature years, updated with valuable new material from the recently opened Frank Lloyd Wright Archives. "Fascinating"–*The New York Times*. 116 illustrations. 128pp. 9¼ x 10¾. 27430-6

PHOTOGRAPHIC SKETCHBOOK OF THE CIVIL WAR, Alexander Gardner. 100 photos taken on field during the Civil War. Famous shots of Manassas Harper's Ferry, Lincoln, Richmond, slave pens, etc. 244pp. 10⅞ x 8¼. 22731-6

FIVE ACRES AND INDEPENDENCE, Maurice G. Kains. Great back-to-the-land classic explains basics of self-sufficient farming. The one book to get. 95 illustrations. 397pp. 5⅜ x 8½. 20974-1

SONGS OF EASTERN BIRDS, Dr. Donald J. Borror. Songs and calls of 60 species most common to eastern U.S.: warblers, woodpeckers, flycatchers, thrushes, larks, many more in high-quality recording. Cassette and manual 99912-2

A MODERN HERBAL, Margaret Grieve. Much the fullest, most exact, most useful compilation of herbal material. Gigantic alphabetical encyclopedia, from aconite to zedoary, gives botanical information, medical properties, folklore, economic uses, much else. Indispensable to serious reader. 161 illustrations. 888pp. 6½ x 9¼. 2-vol. set. (Available in U.S. only.) Vol. I: 22798-7
Vol. II: 22799-5

HIDDEN TREASURE MAZE BOOK, Dave Phillips. Solve 34 challenging mazes accompanied by heroic tales of adventure. Evil dragons, people-eating plants, blood-thirsty giants, many more dangerous adversaries lurk at every twist and turn. 34 mazes, stories, solutions. 48pp. 8¼ x 11. 24566-7

LETTERS OF W. A. MOZART, Wolfgang A. Mozart. Remarkable letters show bawdy wit, humor, imagination, musical insights, contemporary musical world; includes some letters from Leopold Mozart. 276pp. 5⅜ x 8½. 22859-2

BASIC PRINCIPLES OF CLASSICAL BALLET, Agrippina Vaganova. Great Russian theoretician, teacher explains methods for teaching classical ballet. 118 illustrations. 175pp. 5⅜ x 8½. 22036-2

THE JUMPING FROG, Mark Twain. Revenge edition. The original story of The Celebrated Jumping Frog of Calaveras County, a hapless French translation, and Twain's hilarious "retranslation" from the French. 12 illustrations. 66pp. 5⅜ x 8½. 22686-7

BEST REMEMBERED POEMS, Martin Gardner (ed.). The 126 poems in this superb collection of 19th- and 20th-century British and American verse range from Shelley's "To a Skylark" to the impassioned "Renascence" of Edna St. Vincent Millay and to Edward Lear's whimsical "The Owl and the Pussycat." 224pp. 5⅜ x 8½. 27165-X

COMPLETE SONNETS, William Shakespeare. Over 150 exquisite poems deal with love, friendship, the tyranny of time, beauty's evanescence, death and other themes in language of remarkable power, precision and beauty. Glossary of archaic terms. 80pp. 5³⁄₁₆ x 8¼. 26686-9

THE BATTLES THAT CHANGED HISTORY, Fletcher Pratt. Eminent historian profiles 16 crucial conflicts, ancient to modern, that changed the course of civilization. 352pp. 5⅜ x 8½. 41129-X

THE WIT AND HUMOR OF OSCAR WILDE, Alvin Redman (ed.). More than 1,000 ripostes, paradoxes, wisecracks: Work is the curse of the drinking classes; I can resist everything except temptation; etc. 258pp. 5⅜ x 8½. 20602-5

SHAKESPEARE LEXICON AND QUOTATION DICTIONARY, Alexander Schmidt. Full definitions, locations, shades of meaning in every word in plays and poems. More than 50,000 exact quotations. 1,485pp. 6½ x 9¼. 2-vol. set.
Vol. 1: 22726-X
Vol. 2: 22727-8

SELECTED POEMS, Emily Dickinson. Over 100 best-known, best-loved poems by one of America's foremost poets, reprinted from authoritative early editions. No comparable edition at this price. Index of first lines. 64pp. 5³⁄₁₆ x 8¼. 26466-1

THE INSIDIOUS DR. FU-MANCHU, Sax Rohmer. The first of the popular mystery series introduces a pair of English detectives to their archnemesis, the diabolical Dr. Fu-Manchu. Flavorful atmosphere, fast-paced action, and colorful characters enliven this classic of the genre. 208pp. 5³⁄₁₆ x 8¼. 29898-1

THE MALLEUS MALEFICARUM OF KRAMER AND SPRENGER, translated by Montague Summers. Full text of most important witchhunter's "bible," used by both Catholics and Protestants. 278pp. 6⅝ x 10. 22802-9

SPANISH STORIES/CUENTOS ESPAÑOLES: A Dual-Language Book, Angel Flores (ed.). Unique format offers 13 great stories in Spanish by Cervantes, Borges, others. Faithful English translations on facing pages. 352pp. 5⅜ x 8½. 25399-6

GARDEN CITY, LONG ISLAND, IN EARLY PHOTOGRAPHS, 1869–1919, Mildred H. Smith. Handsome treasury of 118 vintage pictures, accompanied by carefully researched captions, document the Garden City Hotel fire (1899), the Vanderbilt Cup Race (1908), the first airmail flight departing from the Nassau Boulevard Aerodrome (1911), and much more. 96pp. 8⅞ x 11¾. 40669-5

OLD QUEENS, N.Y., IN EARLY PHOTOGRAPHS, Vincent F. Seyfried and William Asadorian. Over 160 rare photographs of Maspeth, Jamaica, Jackson Heights, and other areas. Vintage views of DeWitt Clinton mansion, 1939 World's Fair and more. Captions. 192pp. 8⅞ x 11. 26358-4

CAPTURED BY THE INDIANS: 15 Firsthand Accounts, 1750-1870, Frederick Drimmer. Astounding true historical accounts of grisly torture, bloody conflicts, relentless pursuits, miraculous escapes and more, by people who lived to tell the tale. 384pp. 5⅜ x 8½. 24901-8

THE WORLD'S GREAT SPEECHES (Fourth Enlarged Edition), Lewis Copeland, Lawrence W. Lamm, and Stephen J. McKenna. Nearly 300 speeches provide public speakers with a wealth of updated quotes and inspiration–from Pericles' funeral oration and William Jennings Bryan's "Cross of Gold Speech" to Malcolm X's powerful words on the Black Revolution and Earl of Spenser's tribute to his sister, Diana, Princess of Wales. 944pp. 5⅜ x 8⅜. 40903-1

THE BOOK OF THE SWORD, Sir Richard F. Burton. Great Victorian scholar/adventurer's eloquent, erudite history of the "queen of weapons"–from prehistory to early Roman Empire. Evolution and development of early swords, variations (sabre, broadsword, cutlass, scimitar, etc.), much more. 336pp. 6⅛ x 9¼. 25434-8

AUTOBIOGRAPHY: The Story of My Experiments with Truth, Mohandas K. Gandhi. Boyhood, legal studies, purification, the growth of the Satyagraha (nonviolent protest) movement. Critical, inspiring work of the man responsible for the freedom of India. 480pp. 5⅜ x 8½. (Available in U.S. only.) 24593-4

CELTIC MYTHS AND LEGENDS, T. W. Rolleston. Masterful retelling of Irish and Welsh stories and tales. Cuchulain, King Arthur, Deirdre, the Grail, many more. First paperback edition. 58 full-page illustrations. 512pp. 5⅜ x 8½. 26507-2

THE PRINCIPLES OF PSYCHOLOGY, William James. Famous long course complete, unabridged. Stream of thought, time perception, memory, experimental methods; great work decades ahead of its time. 94 figures. 1,391pp. 5⅜ x 8½. 2-vol. set.
Vol. I: 20381-6   Vol. II: 20382-4

THE WORLD AS WILL AND REPRESENTATION, Arthur Schopenhauer. Definitive English translation of Schopenhauer's life work, correcting more than 1,000 errors, omissions in earlier translations. Translated by E. F. J. Payne. Total of 1,269pp. 5⅜ x 8½. 2-vol. set. Vol. 1: 21761-2   Vol. 2: 21762-0

MAGIC AND MYSTERY IN TIBET, Madame Alexandra David-Neel. Experiences among lamas, magicians, sages, sorcerers, Bonpa wizards. A true psychic discovery. 32 illustrations. 321pp. 5⅜ x 8½. (Available in U.S. only.) 22682-4

THE EGYPTIAN BOOK OF THE DEAD, E. A. Wallis Budge. Complete reproduction of Ani's papyrus, finest ever found. Full hieroglyphic text, interlinear transliteration, word-for-word translation, smooth translation. 533pp. 6½ x 9¼. 21866-X

MATHEMATICS FOR THE NONMATHEMATICIAN, Morris Kline. Detailed, college-level treatment of mathematics in cultural and historical context, with numerous exercises. Recommended Reading Lists. Tables. Numerous figures. 641pp. 5⅜ x 8½. 24823-2

PROBABILISTIC METHODS IN THE THEORY OF STRUCTURES, Isaac Elishakoff. Well-written introduction covers the elements of the theory of probability from two or more random variables, the reliability of such multivariable structures, the theory of random function, Monte Carlo methods of treating problems incapable of exact solution, and more. Examples. 502pp. 5⅜ x 8½. 40691-1

THE RIME OF THE ANCIENT MARINER, Gustave Doré, S. T. Coleridge. Doré's finest work; 34 plates capture moods, subtleties of poem. Flawless full-size reproductions printed on facing pages with authoritative text of poem. "Beautiful. Simply beautiful."–*Publisher's Weekly.* 77pp. 9¼ x 12. 22305-1

NORTH AMERICAN INDIAN DESIGNS FOR ARTISTS AND CRAFTSPEOPLE, Eva Wilson. Over 360 authentic copyright-free designs adapted from Navajo blankets, Hopi pottery, Sioux buffalo hides, more. Geometrics, symbolic figures, plant and animal motifs, etc. 128pp. 8⅜ x 11. (Not for sale in the United Kingdom.) 25341-4

SCULPTURE: Principles and Practice, Louis Slobodkin. Step-by-step approach to clay, plaster, metals, stone; classical and modern. 253 drawings, photos. 255pp. 8⅛ x 11. 22960-2

THE INFLUENCE OF SEA POWER UPON HISTORY, 1660–1783, A. T. Mahan. Influential classic of naval history and tactics still used as text in war colleges. First paperback edition. 4 maps. 24 battle plans. 640pp. 5⅜ x 8½. 25509-3

CATALOG OF DOVER BOOKS

THE STORY OF THE TITANIC AS TOLD BY ITS SURVIVORS, Jack Winocour (ed.). What it was really like. Panic, despair, shocking inefficiency, and a little heroism. More thrilling than any fictional account. 26 illustrations. 320pp. 5⅜ x 8½.
20610-6

FAIRY AND FOLK TALES OF THE IRISH PEASANTRY, William Butler Yeats (ed.). Treasury of 64 tales from the twilight world of Celtic myth and legend: "The Soul Cages," "The Kildare Pooka," "King O'Toole and his Goose," many more. Introduction and Notes by W. B. Yeats. 352pp. 5⅜ x 8½.
26941-8

BUDDHIST MAHAYANA TEXTS, E. B. Cowell and others (eds.). Superb, accurate translations of basic documents in Mahayana Buddhism, highly important in history of religions. The Buddha-karita of Asvaghosha, Larger Sukhavativyuha, more. 448pp. 5⅜ x 8½.
25552-2

ONE TWO THREE . . . INFINITY: Facts and Speculations of Science, George Gamow. Great physicist's fascinating, readable overview of contemporary science: number theory, relativity, fourth dimension, entropy, genes, atomic structure, much more. 128 illustrations. Index. 352pp. 5⅜ x 8½.
25664-2

EXPERIMENTATION AND MEASUREMENT, W. J. Youden. Introductory manual explains laws of measurement in simple terms and offers tips for achieving accuracy and minimizing errors. Mathematics of measurement, use of instruments, experimenting with machines. 1994 edition. Foreword. Preface. Introduction. Epilogue. Selected Readings. Glossary. Index. Tables and figures. 128pp. 5⅜ x 8½.   40451-X

DALÍ ON MODERN ART: The Cuckolds of Antiquated Modern Art, Salvador Dalí. Influential painter skewers modern art and its practitioners. Outrageous evaluations of Picasso, Cézanne, Turner, more. 15 renderings of paintings discussed. 44 calligraphic decorations by Dalí. 96pp. 5⅜ x 8½. (Available in U.S. only.)   29220-7

ANTIQUE PLAYING CARDS: A Pictorial History, Henry René D'Allemagne. Over 900 elaborate, decorative images from rare playing cards (14th–20th centuries): Bacchus, death, dancing dogs, hunting scenes, royal coats of arms, players cheating, much more. 96pp. 9¼ x 12¼.
29265-7

MAKING FURNITURE MASTERPIECES: 30 Projects with Measured Drawings, Franklin H. Gottshall. Step-by-step instructions, illustrations for constructing handsome, useful pieces, among them a Sheraton desk, Chippendale chair, Spanish desk, Queen Anne table and a William and Mary dressing mirror. 224pp. 8⅛ x 11¼.
29338-6

THE FOSSIL BOOK: A Record of Prehistoric Life, Patricia V. Rich et al. Profusely illustrated definitive guide covers everything from single-celled organisms and dinosaurs to birds and mammals and the interplay between climate and man. Over 1,500 illustrations. 760pp. 7½ x 10⅛.
29371-8

Paperbound unless otherwise indicated. Available at your book dealer, online at **www.doverpublications.com**, or by writing to Dept. GI, Dover Publications, Inc., 31 East 2nd Street, Mineola, NY 11501. For current price information or for free catalogues (please indicate field of interest), write to Dover Publications or log on to **www.doverpublications.com** and see every Dover book in print. Dover publishes more than 500 books each year on science, elementary and advanced mathematics, biology, music, art, literary history, social sciences, and other areas.

9/16 0